Praise

"This is a unique book – there really is nothing like it on the market right now. It provides new CEOs with an excellent toolbox, giving them the resources they need to be successful in their fundraising journey. If you've been lucky enough to attend one of Giuseppe's training sessions, *Winners Have a Story* is a perfect translation of that. It's color- and content-rich, packed with interesting case studies to illustrate his points, and solidly researched. What more can I say? Read this book!"
— **Felice Verduyn-van Weegen**, Partner, LSP: Life Sciences Partners

"Giuseppe's book is a unique combination of inspiring personal stories and deep expertise in the field of health and life sciences. And it's all blended beautifully into a clear, step-by-step guide to creating the perfect fundraising story. One that takes the reader by the hand and guides them through the challenges to be addressed and the pitfalls to be avoided."
— **Ann Beliën, CEO**, Rejuvenate Biomed

"Great read! The book describes exactly how I feel when I listen to CEOs pitching their company. As a life sciences VC, I know what I'm looking for – but expressing that to the presenting CEOs is another thing altogether. Giuseppe's book is a valuable read, not only for fundraising CEOs but for anyone who

wants to share their ideas with a bigger audience. It is also packed with fascinating anecdotes about movies, old Greeks, and inspiring role models. I was gripped throughout every page."
— **Christina Takke**, Co-founder and Managing Partner, V-Bio Ventures

"This book is a must-read for any CEO preparing for fundraising. I only wish that I had read it earlier – because it would have saved me a lot of time and energy. Giuseppe's writing makes this an easy book to consume, and he has a knack for explaining his storytelling method clearly. Read *Winners Have a Story* and like me, start pitching a story that convinces and inspires investors – just way before I did!"
— **Remberto Martis**, CEO, LenioBio

"In health and life sciences, every innovation needs to address the same questions: Will it improve patients' lives? Is it safe? Is there a market for it? But for any startup needing to raise millions, the real questions are: How do I grab the attention of investors? How do I differentiate myself from the competitors? How do I convince investors and partners that we are the next big thing? Having a story that addresses those questions is the CEO's job. Because pitching a clear and compelling story makes the difference between success and failure. And *Winners Have a Story* does a great job of explaining how to do that."
— **Florence Allouche**, Former CEO, SparingVision; President, Myrpharm Advisors

"Follow the five principles described in this book and create a story that investors will understand and get excited about. Because CEOs without a story will be forgotten before we even hear about their great product. No story, no glory."

— **Theo Hendriks**, Author, speaker, storyteller

Winners have a story

How CEOs can turn complex science and technology into irresistible fundraising pitches

Giuseppe Marzio, PhD

R^ethink

First published in Great Britain in 2022
by Rethink Press (www.rethinkpress.com)

To my wife Judith and my daughters Sofia and Carmen,
for our unforgettable movie nights eating calzoni

And to Quentin Tarantino,
who will not read it but is so much part of this book

Contents

Introduction

As a business leader in the health and life sciences, you are developing products that will make the world a better and healthier place. What might be in your way? Perhaps your fundraising takes too long or requires too much effort from you. Perhaps you struggle to take your business to the next level. Or perhaps you feel that your conversations with prospects, partners, and collaborators are not going in the direction you want.

You've seen other CEOs in your sector become a honeypot for investors and the darlings of the media, yet you know your big idea, your science, and your product are better than theirs. That hurts, doesn't it? But rather than pouring salt in the wound, what can you do about it?

The health and life sciences sector has become an increasingly crowded and noisy space. The industry has been receiving so much attention: because of the COVID-19 pandemic, of course, but also the new medical, economic, and societal challenges posed by aging and its associated diseases.

There are hundreds of startups, all vying for attention and competing with established companies and big corporations. Companies that don't have a clear and compelling story to share are ignored. You may have great science, but to get it noticed, you need to tell a compelling story. That's how you create excitement, get people motivated, make them eager to work with you – make them want to invest in you.

It is a complex arena for CEOs of health and life sciences companies to get noticed. And as they grow their business, they will encounter three significant problems, whether they are conscious of it or not.

First of all, investors seem to ignore them. CEOs reach out to venture capitalists (VCs), send their decks, and present at countless conferences but somehow fail to get invited to pitch. Or when they do get invited, reactions are lukewarm; there is no follow-up meeting, or VCs ask them to come back when they have better data, clearer validation, more substantial intellectual property.

Second, CEOs struggle to get the attention of potential industry partners. Big pharma players are not that excited about their technology; during business presentations, the wrong kind of questions get asked; and they have difficulty taking the conversation to the next level.

And third, they work hard to attract top talent to their leadership team and their company.

CEOs feel they waste lots of time and effort in these processes.

On the other hand, getting access to investors and a public stage has become easier than ever before. In this hyperconnected world, you are always just one Zoom call away from delivering your best pitch and getting the funding your company needs. Social media allows you to share your story with the right audiences wherever they are, dramatically boosting your story's reach and impact.

I am a scientist turned communications pro with more than twenty years of experience in academia, biotech, and the pharmaceutical sector. In my agency, I have worked with more than a hundred founders and CEOs of health and life science companies and have seen the impact a compelling story has had on their business. Since bringing their great ideas to life with an irresistible story, they have gone on to raise hundreds of millions of dollars, close high-value deals, and take their organization to the next level. I have witnessed first-hand how CEOs with a clear and compelling story win the attention of investors and secure the funding they need. I have seen them turn into inspiring leaders and sought-after keynote speakers who stand out from the crowd and gain authority and the respect of their peers.

I have written *Winners Have a Story* to guide you through the necessary steps to create your own story. And as the CEO, the company story is your responsibility. It is not something you can delegate to your communication department or management team. Because the story and the strategy are the same thing, refining your story means refining your strategy.

Setting up a successful company today takes a different set of skills than those required fifteen to twenty years ago. The ability to tell a clear and compelling story is now more crucial than ever: investors, partners, and employees all expect to hear the story from you, the CEO, because they know that a good story is a powerful predictor of success.

The story you pitch creates both an emotional and logical connection to your mission in the audience. It helps investors understand what lies at the heart of your business. It shows more prominent firms that your strategy and values align with their own and that working with you is mutually beneficial. It attracts the best scientists, business developers, and patent attorneys to join you in this adventure. They'll feel compelled to make your company a big success – and together make the world a healthier place.

This book will show you how to craft a compelling story that will clarify your strategy and convey the value of your product, company, and big idea, bringing together your potential investors' logical and emotional brains. I will introduce you to my tried and tested method for building a successful fundraising story, derived from the storytelling principles used for millennia that still form the basis for every popular book, movie, and series – the StoryPitch™ model:

- As CEO, you need to be the owner of the story.

- You need Clarity in your strategy as the first step to success.

- You need to Construct a story, because story and strategy are the same thing.

- You need effective Communication assets to share your story and convey the value of your big idea.

- You need to aim to Change the world, not just pitch your product.

After reading this book, you will have the tools you need to create a compelling, engaging, and inspiring fundraising story for your company and your product. You will learn to turn complex science and technology into a narrative that is simple enough for investors to understand and powerful enough to excite them.

Let's be straight. No story can ever make you success-ful if your idea is not commercially interesting, if the science supporting your product is patchy, or if you lack the motivation necessary to own your company's narrative. But if you believe in your product, technol-ogy, and vision, this book will show you how to create a story that will become your most valuable business tool.

And once you have that, you will see that something magical happens, both inside and outside of your company. You will notice that your management team will start getting you. They will finally understand your excitement, they will start believing in your vision, and they will become valuable ambassadors in your fundraising journey. Your employees will start getting you. They will become motivated and com-mitted to your company. And importantly, investors will start getting you. Your conversations with them will change and they will begin to feel part of your mission instead of just money-givers.

This is the unique thing about good stories: they spread fast.

This book will help you join the ranks of successful entrepreneurs creating and sharing inspiring stories about their product, company, and vision. I've seen what happens once these CEOs get their story right: they recruit better, their public profile strengthens, and they are more likely to deliver a positive investment return. They have a competitive advantage in every area, not just fundraising.

Crafting a clear and compelling story takes time and dedication. But bringing your story to life is one of the most significant investments you can make for yourself and your company. When you get your story right, everything else will follow.

Winners have a story. What's yours?

PART ONE
SUCCESS STARTS WITH A GREAT STORY

When we hear the word "story," many different things come to mind. The book your mother read to you hundreds of times before going to bed. Your favorite movie, the one you never get tired of watching. Or perhaps that inspiring TED presentation that changed your view of the world forever. Stories are certainly all these things and much more.

Stories are also closely linked to business success. Storytelling has become a core skill for twenty-first-century business leaders. From Oprah Winfrey to Richard Branson to Elon Musk, today's most successful entrepreneurs are those who excel at creating and sharing inspiring stories about their product, company, and vision.

You can do that, too. Let's start by understanding how stories work.

ONE
Why You Need A Story

We all know them. The CEOs with a great story.

They get invited to give keynote presentations. The media love them. They find it easy to get funding, close partnership deals, and attract great talents to their organization. How do they do it?

The new battleground of funding

In the past, most of the pitching in the health and life sciences sector was done by the academics or scientists who had made the original discovery. They often aimed to build standalone labs, hire more scientists and technicians, and advance their scientific observation into a real drug discovery through venture capital funding.

Although that still happens, today pitching is the job of the CEO (yes, you) and in the coming chapters, we'll investigate what that means.

Cash is essential for more than research and development costs. It not only allows startups to function and grow, but it also provides a competitive advantage, helping CEOs to hire in critical roles, including the best scientists, business developers, and legal experts. Considering the fierce competition and overall costs necessary to bring a product to clinical development, it's a rare startup that is not trying to raise money.

The good news is that there are lots of investors hoping to give money to the right startup. Today, the life sciences and biotech sectors are awash with cash, partly because the COVID-19 pandemic focused global attention on public health. And getting in front of investors has become much easier with many encounters and first-time meetings taking place virtually.

The bad news is that fundraising is still a long, complex, and ego-deflating process. While there is more money to fight over, competition is fierce. Companies from very different disciplines are now competing in the same arena. Besides big pharma, giant tech companies like Alphabet, Amazon, Apple, and Microsoft are accelerating their pursuit of the healthcare market and reshaping the expectations of the sector.

You might have great technology and a fantastic new product, but to get the company moving forward, you need a story that gets you noticed. If you don't, it's hard to get people motivated to join you to work on your product and to give you money to develop it.

A story is what makes investors write checks. They have to find the idea compelling enough to be persuaded that your team can realize the vision, and that the opportunity on offer is genuine and sufficiently interesting. CEOs must be ready to convey all this to raise cash.

INSIDE STORY – KEY STAGES OF STARTUP FINANCING

Fundraising is critical for the success of most companies, from the moment they are founded to the time they go public. Based on the stage of the company growth and the amount of capital needed, the following terms are generally used:

- Pre-seed is the earliest funding stage, although not used by every startup. Companies at this stage often consist of only a few team members, perhaps just the company founder. Funding is needed to get the company through the first critical steps, like hiring team members, covering initial research costs, and preparing for the next funding stage.

- The seed round is generally the first serious money in. It can come from various sources, including grants, non-profit organizations, and angel investors. The funds are needed to validate the idea and conduct initial proof-of-concept studies. On average, startups will raise anywhere from $100,000 to a couple of million dollars in this initial funding round.

- Series A is the first institutional round of financing after seed capital runs out. Funding is provided mainly by VCs, alone or in syndicates. A representative of the lead investor generally takes a seat on the board.

- Series B/C/D rounds are required to sustain the company's growth, finance clinical development, and close a licensing deal with pharma or to an initial public offering (IPO). Funding can be raised from VCs and corporate investors.

The amount of capital raised at each step depends on the product type, eg, biopharmaceuticals, medical devices, diagnostics.

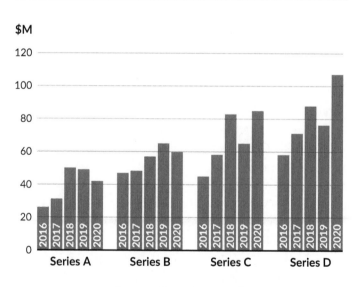

Average financing round,
Biopharma and Therapeutic platforms[1]

This is a story world

We live in a world of stories. Stories permeate everything we do, and people are used to receiving information in this form.

The term "stories" has pervaded our culture. If you do an Ngram (word frequency) search on Google, you will see that the use of the word "story" has dramatically increased in the past fifty years. For comparison, the search for "commercial" and "marketing" has decreased.

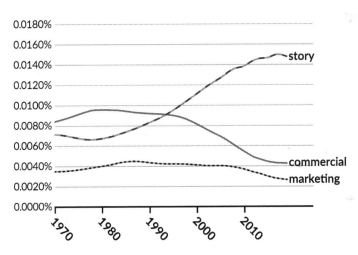

Ngram search: "story," "commercial," and "marketing"[2]

The word "story" first referred to narratives in spoken word, then in print in both fiction and non-fiction forms, such as news items. Later came the movies, TV series and, most recently, social media. Now we curate our own stories, highlighting our lives on Instagram,

Facebook, LinkedIn, and whatever the next platform will be. We not only share personal stories, but also brand stories about our products and vision. These are often highly visual and have the potential to reach hundreds of thousands – sometimes millions – of people.

The new generation of young entrepreneurs find it natural to express themselves through visual stories and grew up learning the skills they need. You can see these young storyteller CEOs at conferences, captivating audiences with powerful and visually arresting presentations, while some of their older peers struggle with something that looks like a slide deck from the nineties.

There is also a new generation of investors who are used to and appreciate a high level of visual storytelling.

To stand out from the crowd and be heard by them, you need to up your story game.

The journey of a thousand pitches

The journey of a health and life sciences CEO is the journey of a thousand pitches. No matter where your company is on its ladder, no matter how mature or how new your product is, your job – it can feel like your only job – is to pitch continuously about it.

Progressing an idea from the lab to clinical development takes many years and is expensive. Even more time is required to get it to market, with the cost shooting up from a few million dollars to a few billion. The whole process can take a decade or more. Throughout this period, you must keep the attention of investors, partners, and colleagues sharply focused on your vision and they should stay as excited about it as you. Otherwise, you are going to fail.

Without funding, most companies in this sector will fail. The capital needed to take a health and life sciences startup to profitability is well beyond the ability of founders and their friends and family to finance. As CEO, you'll be pitching to investors to seed fund your idea. You'll sit in front of venture capitalists again for Series A and for an extended Series A to take your discovery to clinical trials, then Series B and Series C to get to the next stage. Along the way you will also pitch to possible partners, the press and, of course, your employees.

Not surprisingly, investors put a high value on the ability of a CEO to tell a clear and compelling story about their big idea. They are also looking for a CEO with the strategy to turn their idea into a huge commercial success.

Your story is not about marketing. This is a mistake many people make. No, your story is your strategy, and your strategy is your story. If you make your story better, you make your strategy better by clarifying and refining it.

The CEO's three biggest problems

As you've probably discovered by now, life's not easy when you're the CEO of a startup or scale-up company. It's a struggle getting in front of investors. The meeting you had with a big pharma company just got canceled. Research is going slow in the lab and you've already spent far too much time interviewing people who just aren't up to the job.

You're not alone. Speak to any health and life sciences CEO, and you'll discover they've all experienced the kind of challenges you're facing right now.

There is one solution that will solve the biggest challenges faced by growing companies like yours: you need a strategic story. This is a high-level narrative that clarifies your strategy and conveys the value of your science, your product, and your company. Nail it, and that's when you'll start to see results. This isn't about including a story in your pitch. Your strategic story should *be* your pitch.

INSIDE STORY – WHAT IS A STORY?

The *Oxford English Dictionary* gives three definitions of the word "story":

- An account of imaginary or real people and events told for entertainment, eg, "The novel has a good story"

- An account of past events in someone's life or in the development of something, eg, "The story of modern farming"
- The commercial prospects or circumstances of a particular company, eg, "The investors' flight to profitable businesses with solid stories"

It is this last meaning of the word "story" that comes the closest to our subject in this book.

A story is a tool to convey an idea in a way that maximizes its chances of success. It provides clarity, powers the idea forward, and protects it from criticism. Storytelling is not all fireworks, meaningful anecdotes, and pulling on heartstrings. It's concrete and analytical, and it's the simplest way to connect with your audiences, whether they are investors, clients, or partners.

As legendary entrepreneur Richard Branson says, storytelling is the way to get your point of view across, differentiate your brand, and work out new ideas. "Today, if you want to succeed as an entrepreneur, you also have to be a storyteller."[3]

While your story is not about marketing, your pitch can certainly be a marketing tool. Emotionally captivating stories can convince employees, advisers, and investors to commit to being part of building your strategic vision.

CASE STUDY – DREAMING BIG

A spin-out company of a global corporation was launched to develop a new technology platform, which had the potential to revolutionize the drug development market, thanks to its efficiency and broad applicability. Initially, the CEO positioned the company around the technology, pitching a story about technological innovation and superiority to competitors.

But soon the CEO, his team, and his close advisers realized that this narrative was limiting their ambition and not reflecting the reasons why they had founded and joined the company in the first place: to solve one of the world's biggest challenges, and to solve it on a global scale.

For the new story, they started by describing their big dream, where they dared to position their small startup at the level of global organizations and health foundations that shared their vision. Their new pitch resonated with many audiences, from the very health foundations they compared themselves to, to leading investors.

The CEO was invited to meet global leaders, won prestigious prizes, and eventually closed an above-expectation Series A funding round with a major VC firm. But the most important prize was the motivation and commitment that the new story brought to the organization.

EXERCISE – THE STORY PEOPLE TELL ABOUT YOU NOW

What is the story circulating about you and your company right now? It's important to understand where you're starting from, so that you have a reference point from which to measure your progress later. It will also be such a pleasant surprise to revisit your current story when you have your new one ready to share.

- Start by collecting five versions of your story that are circulating right now. Ask five people this very simple question: "If you were to introduce my company to a colleague, what would you say in one sentence?"
- Make sure you choose five people with different viewpoints:
  1. A member of your leadership team
  2. An employee, perhaps a scientist
  3. An investor who has already invested in you, or an investor you know personally and trust
  4. A fellow CEO working in another company
  5. An adviser, somebody in your supervisory board
- Write these five short stories down and then add your own, perhaps copied from the opening slide of your pitch deck or the landing page of your website.

What do you see? Are the statements all the same? Are they very different? What is the common theme emerging? Who has made a statement closest to your message?

How would you rate the consistency of your current story? Give yourself one point for each of the statements that is consistent with the story you tell. How many points out of five did you score?

Come back to this exercise at the end of the book and repeat it regularly every few weeks. How is your new story doing? Is the consistency improving? Are your different audiences getting the same story now?

Summary

The world of fundraising has changed dramatically in the last couple of years. The COVID-19 crisis has transformed the industry, creating immense opportunities for institutions and investors to drive healthcare innovation.

In the health and life sciences sector, the post-pandemic sense of urgency and market opportunity is fostering an era of unprecedented growth. The need for increased research, diagnostic, and manufacturing capabilities is high on the agenda of politicians and industry executives alike.

With the global attention focused on the importance of the sector for the well-being of society and its citizens, investors are prepared to invest heavily in health and life sciences. Venture capitalists are raising record amounts of cash to pour into life sciences businesses, to gain exposure to a sector that has been in the spotlight during the pandemic.

At the same time, competition is fierce. As first-time meetings have mostly moved online and getting in front of investors is technically easier than ever, rising above the noise has become hard. The separation of different sectors is now fading, bringing CEOs from diverse fields to compete in the same space.

And a new generation of founders is entering the scene – a breed of young entrepreneurs who take stories and visual communication for granted as part of their world.

If you are struggling to get funded, find the right partners, and attract talent; perhaps the problem is that your story is not exciting enough. Read on for how to fix it.

TWO

Nobody Said It Was Easy

As a CEO, you probably already have a lot of experience presenting your big idea, product, or company. Perhaps you have done one or more fundraising rounds with some success. Now you want to take your pitch to the next level, starting with your story.

If you have read the previous chapter, you will be convinced of the importance of a clear story for the success of your business, especially in the startup and growth phase. But change is hard, and that is also true when it comes to embracing your story. Sometimes it's your environment that makes it difficult for you, sometimes it's you.

This chapter will explore some of the challenges and objections you are likely to encounter when you try to commit to your story and get others on board, and how you can overcome them.

Objection 1

"I don't need a story because investors make decisions based on facts."

Investing in your product or company is a decision that involves millions of dollars. We expect investors to make such important decisions based on facts and logic. It is not surprising that most CEOs pitching to investors try to appeal to their rational side. This is the approach that they find easiest. They see themselves as rational beings, often with PhDs and MBAs. They cannot imagine that such big decisions could be swayed by anything other than sheer logic and deep analysis of the information available.

But it turns out that logic might not be the best way to convince investors to fund your company. Because decision-making isn't logical – it's emotional, according to neuroscience.

Over a century ago, Swiss psychiatrist and psychoanalyst Carl Jung discovered that each person receives and processes information in four ways: thinking, feeling, knowing, and sensing.[4] Each of us has a preferred mode, although we use all four to different extents:

- **Thinkers** use data. They study facts and figures. They analyze and deduce.

- **Feelers** consider their emotions, focus on how they feel about something to find the way that "feels right."

- **Knowers** go by intuition. They may not actually know how they made the decision, but they are sure it's the right one.

- **Sensors** will rely heavily on input from their senses to inform them of the right choice.

Imagine you are considering where to go on holiday. If you are a thinker, you are likely to study options, compare prices, read reviews. This process often takes a lot of time and energy – I know this very well, because I am a thinker too.

Feelers recall past holidays they enjoyed very much. They ask themselves, "What do I feel like doing this year?" They read reviews too, and spend a lot of time gathering information, but focus on the overall impression they get, rather than on specific sites or hotels.

Knowers know exactly where they want to go and what they want to do. They don't have time to waste, especially not discussing their plans with feelers and thinkers.

Sensors will look at the pictures of the location and read stories of other people who have been there before them. They will try to experience the holiday ahead of time.

This model has been tried and tested millions of times and is still the basis of personality metrics.

And then the interesting part: when it's time to decide and click the "reserve" button, something unexpected happens. Neuroscientist Antonio Damasio made a ground-breaking discovery about this at the beginning of this century. Damasio worked with patients with injury or disease affecting their amygdala, the brain region that plays a crucial role in responding to feelings such as fear and aggression. People with this damage behave normally but are unable to feel emotions. He discovered that they had something else in common: they couldn't make decisions.[5] They understood that they had a choice, but they found it very challenging to make even the most straightforward decision, such as what to eat. They couldn't decide what was in their own best interest. You could say they lacked good judgment. When emotion was impaired, so was decision-making.

Without the filtering provided by emotions, the data sets for any given decision – whether it's what to get for lunch or whom to marry – would be overwhelming. If you think about it, every choice we make has potentially so many consequences. How do we evaluate all the pros and cons and arrive at a decision? Logic is not enough. The critical step is always made at the emotional level.

So emotions are essential at the point when we have to choose, even when we believe we are making logical decisions. This is true even for investors, when it's time to decide whether they want to invest or not.

A story in this context works similarly to a negotiation process. You don't tell your opponent what to think or what's best. You help them discover for themselves what feels right and most advantageous to them. Their ultimate decision is based on self-interest: "I want this. This is good for my people and me." That's emotional.

Objection 2

"I don't need a story because the data should speak for itself."

Many health and life sciences CEOs have a scientific background. Perhaps they are involved in the scientific breakthrough, the drug, or the technology, or maybe they played an essential role in making it happen. "Do not tamper with data" is the most important mantra for scientists. The worst thing a scientist can do is misinterpret data or mislead the public in its interpretation. This is reflected in how scientists present data at conferences or to their peers. But this attitude towards data and scientific integrity also influences them when presenting their ideas to investors. And even those who do not have a scientific background can show enormous zeal and commitment to relying on data to communicate their message.

In fact, data doesn't speak for itself. You have to do it. You are the voice of your data. Your results are never self-explanatory. They need to be put in context to be fully appreciated.

The behavioral economist Dan Ariely describes how people don't appreciate things by their face value. They determine their value based on context: "We don't have an internal value meter that tells us how much things are worth. Rather, we focus on the relative advantage of one thing over another and estimate value accordingly."[6] In other words, we put our options into context. We can't help but evaluate everything in relation to what we see around us.

This is true not only for choosing material things, like a new car or a new bike, but also for experiences like a holiday or a movie and emotional things, like friends or attitudes or points of view. We compare everything. We need context, and story can help to provide that context. A story puts your data into a bigger picture, one that gives it more significant value to the listener.

This is something that brands know well. We value a pair of shoes or a pair of sunglasses not only because of the technical specs (how well they keep our feet dry or shield our eyes), but because we have a particular story in our heads that compares them to all the other shoes or sunglasses we could choose. We want the story – perhaps the story of success, perhaps the story of being attractive – that these shoes or sunglasses have and that the other options don't.

When it comes to writing your story, for example, you could position your new anticancer drug as an innovative technological innovation: "We develop next-generation anticancer therapy based on [fill in your technology]." Or you could contextualize it as an exciting new medical trend: "We develop precision medicine therapies for cancer." You could even present it as an unresolved therapeutic challenge: "We develop therapies for hard-to-treat solid tumors." However you decide to tell it, set yourself apart with a story that puts you in the best context.

Objection 3

"I don't need a story because I don't have time to tell a story."

It feels natural to tell a beautiful and compelling story when you have all the time in the world for it, such as when you are invited to give a keynote presentation, or you have an hour-long meeting with investors. But what about other times, like when you meet somebody for a couple of minutes during a coffee break, or you have a ten-minute slot with your investor to discuss your product and its scientific basis?

How can you make time for a story? Or should you even try? Should you dive straight into the data, the financials, the projections? And is there a formula to help you understand how much emotion you should put in your pitch and how much logic?

Every interaction you have with your audience, whether they are investors or a big pharma company who would like to partner with you, consider it a personal one. Sometimes the first time you meet someone new, you know right away that you want to spend the rest of your life with them. You want them to know everything about you. But most of the time, you just don't know that. You have to take the relationship in small steps. You often start by building an emotional connection. Do you like this person?

In the early phase of your relationship, you need to create connection and trust. And that is not something that is based on logic. It's emotional. So if you have only limited time and you are at the beginning of your interaction, by all means start with the story, and give only enough content to take the conversation to the next stage. (We'll look at how you can do this in more detail in Chapter 7.) If you have already established a relationship with your contact or your audience, you can be lighter on the emotional connection and emphasize the facts. If you have known each other for a long time, it's easier to jump straight into the facts, the science, and the financials.

Objection 4

"I don't need a story because my product is years away from the market."

When we think about inspiring CEOs who use the power of storytelling to propel the success of their companies, certain people come to mind – Steve Jobs, Jeff Bezos, Elon Musk. But none of these people are working in health and life sciences, where taking a product to market can take ten years or more. Sometimes the product never reaches the market.

This is an objection I often hear from CEOs: "How can I pitch my product – how can I pitch a compelling story about my product – if I don't have a product yet? I only have a great idea, and some promising results that need to be proven in the clinic."

My answer to this is that the further away you are from the reality of having an approved product, the more critical it is to have a compelling story.

Think of a story as a bridge that takes your audience from one side of a river to the other, from where you are now to where you want to be. The wider the river is to cross, the more critical the bridge becomes. They will never get there without the bridge.

Think about the billionaire Elon Musk and his current adventure, SpaceX. He first pitched his idea of making humans an interplanetary species in 2016. Mr. Musk began his presentation with the existential concern over Earth's long-term future, and the need to set up a civilization beyond our planet to safeguard the species.[7] Did he have a multiplanetary mission to Mars back then? Of course not. That will take years, possibly a decade or more. But his story allowed us to bridge the gap – a huge one – between his vision and the reality his product will help create. The bigger the vision, the more important the story becomes. In Musk's own words: "I can't think of anything more exciting than going out there and being among the stars."[8]

A few decades before Elon Musk's SpaceX program, another big dream of space travel was born. On 12 September 1962, President John F. Kennedy stood in front of a crowd of roughly 35,000 at Rice University and declared that the United States would put "a man on the moon" "before the end of this decade."[9]

The space race had become heated between the Soviets and the United States. Just six weeks before JFK's speech, Yuri Gagarin, a Soviet cosmonaut, became the first person in space. The pressure was on for America to send astronauts into the final frontier.

The purpose of the speech wasn't just to rally and inspire the nation to reach for the moon. It was to explain to the American people why the Apollo space program needed to be a high priority, which would allow for a "boost" in federal funds. It was almost a fundraising pitch, not so different from Elon Musk's Tesla Powerwall pitch (which I will analyze in depth in Chapter 9). The pitch was successful. The US government committed $25 billion to the Apollo program, equivalent to over $100 billion today. Seven years after the speech, Neil Armstrong set foot on the moon. It was more than a historic moment. It was a global victory.

Objection 5

"I don't need a story because I need to work on my deck first."

Creating a compelling story for your company takes time. In my experience, it can take anything between a couple of weeks to a month to create a story that you feel confident enough to share with your board, your colleagues, investors, and the world.

If you're not convinced that you have the time to work on your story, just consider this. How much time do you, your management team, or your colleagues spend on preparing presentations for meetings and pitches to investors? In my experience, CEOs put a lot of time and energy into refining and perfecting their presentation: changing the sequence of the slides, adding new slides, modifying titles, often working on a new deck for each meeting.

Well, having a clear story will save you time, lots of it. Because once you have created the story, the message you share will be the same for every audience and in every situation. So you won't have to make a new deck every time you go to a different event, or present to a different audience. The story stays the same, although the focus changes.

You could choose to tell an urgency- and emotion-driven story, a content-driven story, or a reputation-driven story, depending on who your audience is and the stage of your interaction with them. We'll discuss this more in Chapter 3, The four basic elements of every compelling story.

Resist the temptation to fixate on the slide deck and think about the story later. Making slides can be a never-ending project. You can always create new decks, new slides, show more results. But how do you manage all that information without the sound structure that a story gives you? Make sure you have a clear story first, then work on the slides. Your audience will be eternally grateful.

Summary

Change is never easy. You have been doing your pitching for some time with some success. You might find it hard to switch to a story-based pitch, even if you're convinced of its importance for the success of your fundraising, and your business. You find objections get in the way when the time comes to commit to creating a story.

One of the most common objections to storytelling is that investors make decisions based on facts. Of course, investors are focused on delivering a return on their investment and they are interested in understanding the scientific basis of your product and your solution.

But investors are also human beings, so there is a crucial emotional element to the decision-making process. Even when investors start the process by taking in your information, in the end, their final decision is influenced by emotion. And data doesn't speak with that voice. So don't hide behind science and information – data will never speak for itself as well as you can speak about it.

Your story is what allows you to put the data into context. Connecting your science to an external reference is the best way to increase the value of your product in the minds of your audience. A story creates that reference. It puts your product in the context of something else, perhaps the successes of pre-existing products, or other innovations in medicine that have already been developed.

Most importantly, a lot of effort goes into fundraising and preparing for pitches and presentations. Having a clear story will allow you to save time and energy that you can then dedicate to your business.

Likely, your product is a decade or more away from reaching patients and bringing a return for investors. Perhaps you are many years away from an IPO or being bought by big pharma. But the further you must travel, the more important your story becomes. This is because the story is the bridge that allows your audience to cross time and space, and experience today the feeling of future success.

THREE

How Stories Work

You might not be fundraising right now, but whoever you are talking to about your science, company, and vision is an investor, because they invest their time and attention in what you have to say. Any opportunity to share your story is one you should take.

But before you start creating your fundraising story, it's worth understanding what makes stories such an effective tool to connect with your audience. First, let's look at what happens when your story is not working in your favor.

Why investors say no

If you're a life science startup, not getting venture capital funding can be a critical barrier to success.

And we're not just talking about missing out on money. VCs provide vital expertise and guidance during the most critical moments in the life of a young company.

Investors say no for many reasons. Typical reasons are that they feel your science is too early, your development plan too risky, or that the market is either too small or too crowded.

Often there are deeper and more complex reasons. From my many professional encounters with VCs, I've identified four recurring reasons why companies fail to win their backing. The surprise is that none of these pitfalls have to do with science or technology or quality of ideas.

Reason 1: Not urgent

You have an innovative product, with a vast market opportunity and an experienced team. Guess what? Most founders and CEOs say they have those too.

So you'll hear, "Come back in six months when you have more data, more traction, more IP, more—" You get the idea. You're back to square one. Ouch.

Maybe what you're missing is urgency. Do you have a compelling reason why a VC should act now?

Reason 2: Not exciting

Investors hear startup pitches constantly, and sometimes, one pitch is hard to tell apart from the next. Great startups get overlooked because they don't stand out from the crowd.

Perhaps your delivery was poor, or the multitude of slides had the audience nodding off – maybe you struck the wrong note and can't tell why. Investors want to put their money into something exciting, and the best time to win their enthusiasm is during the initial pitch. Only the phenomenal few pitches will clinch that deal.

Reason 3: Not credible

No matter how stellar your pitch or unique your product, it can be destroyed by a lack of credibility.

Lacking the right credentials or not being trustworthy will kill any founder. Let's face it, no one's going to invest in somebody or something that seems a bit sketchy.

Reason 4: Not clear

This is the problem that does the most damage during fundraising. As Ben Horowitz, the legendary entrepreneur and co-founder of venture capitalists Andreessen Horowitz, says: "The company story is the company strategy."[10] Companies that don't have a clear story generally don't have a clear strategy.

If you can overcome these four challenges, you will eliminate most of the obstacles to creating a winning fundraising story. So how do you do that? It turns out that each of these challenges is related to one of the four basic elements of persuasive communication, first identified in ancient Greece. Use these and you have a good chance of pitching an irresistible story. Let's look at them in more detail.

The four basic elements of every compelling story

If you want to create a powerful fundraising pitch, persuasive business presentation, or inspiring TED Talk, where do you start? There are literally thousands of books, blogs, and videos on the subject. In fact, there's so much information on storytelling, it can all feel a bit overwhelming. Wouldn't it be good if there was a way to make it simpler?

In many ancient cultures, the nature and complexity of all matter was explained by breaking it down into simpler substances, such as the four elements of water, earth, fire, and air. OK, we now know that it's actually 118 chemical elements, but that is still a finite number. And this isn't restricted to the natural world.

All the books ever written in the English language have been created using the same twenty-six letters of the alphabet. All chords and melodies in western music have been composed from just twelve different notes. And all the paintings, throughout the world, have been produced from just three primary colors: red, yellow, and blue.

Given a set number of building blocks, it's possible to create an almost infinite number of variations. What are the building blocks that we can use to create the perfect story?

Aristotle's four elements of persuasion

All the great pitches, speeches, and presentations in history were created using just four basic building blocks. They were first defined and documented more than two thousand years ago, by the Greek philosopher Aristotle. They've formed the basis of nearly every public speaking book, article, and blog published since. Understanding what these building blocks are and how to use them is key to transforming your next pitch from informative to persuasive.

| logos | ethos | pathos | kairos |

The four elements of persuasion

Logos

Greek for "word," "reason," and the root of the English word "logic," logos appeals to the audience's rationality. It's the basic ingredient of your pitch – the information you present combined with your logically structured argument.

Investors, analysts, and scientists love this stuff, but don't be too heavy on it with a general audience. If someone says, "I don't get it," it's a sure sign that you need to clarify and simplify your logos. But not incorporating enough of it will leave your idea sounding a little lightweight at best, and, more often, unrealistic and irrelevant.

Reinforce your logos with facts, data, graphs, figures, stats, examples, and best of all, demonstrations. Ever wondered why Steve Jobs went to the trouble of personally live demoing every single product? As Aristotle put it, "Persuasion is clearly a sort of demonstration, since we are most fully persuaded when we consider a thing to have been demonstrated."[11]

Ethos

Ethos, Greek for "character," appeals to the audience's sense of honesty and/or authority. It's about being trustworthy and credible – as in the English word "ethical." No matter how much information you share and how good your argument is, your audience will leave the room unconvinced if you score poorly on ethos. Aristotle described it like this: "Persuasion is achieved by the speaker's personal character, when the speech is so spoken as to make us think him credible."

Ethos is crucial in all your dealings with investors: they need to trust that you, the CEO of the company, have the skills, connections, and competence to grow a successful business. That's why investors expect the CEO to give the pitch. They need to see living proof of the credibility of the product.

Ethos is the difference between a pitch that's informative and one that's convincing. It's the difference between "meh" and "yeah!"

Reinforce your ethos by emphasizing your professional achievements, academic titles, affiliations to respected institutions, important collaborations, as well as having a confident stage presence and tone of voice.

Pathos

Pathos is the Greek word for "emotion," as in the English word "empathy." It's about appealing to your audience's feelings, firing up their emotions and strategically connecting these to elements of your speech. According to Aristotle, "Persuasion may come through the hearers, when the speech stirs their emotions." If the audience connects emotionally to your speech, they will be more likely to agree with your argument and respond to your call to action.

Reinforce your pathos with vivid storytelling and engaging delivery. Use humor, look for common ground, provide strong visuals and striking quotes. Convey complex concepts with imaginative metaphors. Share your vision.

Kairos

Kairos is perhaps the most important building block of your pitch, and the most difficult to work with. Kairos is the ancient Greek word for the right, critical, opportune moment, the "timeliness" of your words or actions. Like an archer preparing to fire an arrow, it takes more than a bow, technique, and strength – there is only one instant, a fleeting moment when an opportunity to shoot appears. Shoot too early or late and you'll miss the target. Get the timing right, and you cannot miss.

Aristotle notes that, "The favor will be great if the recipient is in pressing need, or if the times and the circumstances are important or difficult."

Aristotle ties kairos to the roles of pathos, ethos, and logos, claiming that there are times in each situation when one needs to be utilized over the others. Reinforce your kairos by carefully timing the various elements of your pitch. Know when to show the data and when to create an emotional connection, when to create urgency and when to establish trust. Most importantly, you need to explain why now the timing is right to introduce your innovation. Because having a good idea is not enough. It's your job to show your audience that you have a good idea, and to convince them that now is the right time for it to flourish.

Calibrating the four elements of your pitch

Logos, ethos, pathos, and kairos are needed in every pitch. But how much of each you use depends on the situation. Logos and pathos compete with each other. It's our left brain hemisphere versus our right.

The earlier the stage of your interaction with investors, the more you should rely on creating emotional connection and less on data and information. For example, the first one-minute elevator pitch is all about pathos. You want your audience to get excited about your big idea. Don't overload your pitch with complex data and science. At the other extreme of the spectrum, a long due diligence meeting with investors requires you to discuss data, financials, intellectual property. You already have their buy-in. Make sure the emotional part is limited but not eliminated altogether.

Ethos is the foundation on which your story stands and cannot be left out, or the whole construction will crumble. How much you need of it will depend on the audience and how much trust-building is needed. If you have limited experience as a CEO, perhaps you'll need to emphasize the support you get from a stellar supervisory board. If your innovation is in a very early stage, supporting statements from key opinion leaders or scientific publications from other groups would certainly reinforce its credibility.

Kairos is the spice you add to the recipe, the topping on the cake. It enhances the flavor and supercharges the presentation. But don't overdo it.

Like pathos, the earlier the pitch, the stronger the sense of urgency you'll need to create. Because kairos is such a fundamental component of the narrative, it should always be present in the story you are pitching.

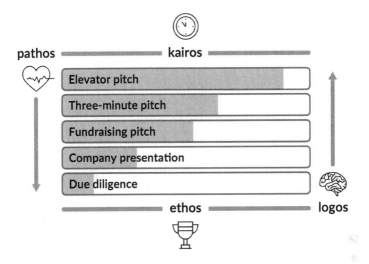

How to calibrate the elements of your pitch

The fifth element: The gift

Inside every successful pitch there is a secret ingredient, which I call the fifth element: the gift. The gift is something that leaves the audience thinking about your words long after they've left the room.

What is it? What is the gift your pitch should be offering to every investor, rousing their interest and fueling their excitement at the same time?

It all starts with a new idea. If your childhood was anything like mine, you will remember the wonders of getting lost in fantastical stories that made the impossible seem possible. One of my favorite books was *Aesop's Fables.*[12]

Aesop, an ancient Greek storyteller, drew on his observations of animals and humans to weave stories that were as entertaining as they were teachable. At the end of each fable was a clear lesson. "The Tortoise and the Hare" was about never giving up. "The Ant and the Grasshopper" was about always being prepared. *Aesop's Fables* showed me, from a young age, that the best stories ignite new perspective, and that new perspective leads to action.

We are addicted to good stories because we learn something from them that we did not know before. And it's not only children who can learn from them. The TED Talks that go viral and reach tens of millions of viewers are the ones that are grounded in a beautiful and unexpected idea. Take Sir Ken Robinson's 2006 TED Talk "Do Schools Kill Creativity?" In the most watched TED Talk of all time, educationalist Sir Ken Robinson made the compelling point that "we don't grow into creativity, we grow out of it. Or rather we get educated out of it." He argued that creativity is as important as literacy and we should treat it as such – a big idea, an inspiring insight that left me thinking about it long after the presentation ended.[13]

Find your gift

The most successful CEOs know that pitching their science and technology isn't enough. They know that simply putting their product at the forefront of their message won't compel, resonate, or incite that shift of perspective. If you want to get your pitch into fighting shape to truly blow investors out of the water, you need to make sure you have something to give.

When Steve Jobs took to the stage at the Macworld Conference in 2007, he didn't talk about a new and improved telephone. He talked about the power of being able to hold a computer in our hand.[14] When Elon Musk gave his Tesla Powerwall presentation in 2015, he didn't talk about a better solar-powered battery. He talked about our Earth being destroyed by pollution, and our responsibility to take action.[15]

Stories are about giving. They're about giving your audience a new idea to think about, and they're about giving them a reason to act.

What is your pitch giving to the audience? Your company's story doesn't need to be ground-breaking. It doesn't need to start a revolution or prompt a new industry. But it does need to bring something new to the conversation. Maybe you're offering:

- A new angle for looking at a disease

- A new vision to helping patients

- A new way to manufacture medicines

Whatever it is, you need to give your audience the gift of new insight, a story they haven't already heard.

INSIDE STORY - WHY A STORY IS MORE THAN A PITCH

While good stories are about giving something, poor pitches limit themselves to asking for something. They don't give the audience something new to think about. They just ask for something from the audience - first, that they commit time to listening, then that they commit money to helping the company flourish.

But no good story is "about" selling. The shift in perspective to the audience feeling moved to invest has to be natural. Action has to be earned.

So give your audience the beautiful, unexpected gift of a new idea. And watch their interest, and their subsequent action, pay dividends.

Spread the word

I am sure this has happened to you before. You read a great book or watch a movie that inspires you. What is the first thing you do?

You probably want to share your experience with a family member, a friend, or a colleague. Social media is all about that, giving us opportunities to share a good story with our network. And the more people we engage with, the better we feel.

Humans are hardwired to love a great story. Stories inspire us. Stories get retold. We remember stories. Perhaps not the exact words, but the feelings they stir in us. The same is true with potential investors. They may forget what your company does or the specifics of your business model, but they will remember how they felt when they heard your company's story.

When CEOs find their story, something magical happens. Not only do investors start to "get" them, but they start sharing themselves. The spread of the story is no longer linear, but exponential. It reaches new audiences without anyone having to pitch it. That is the magic of storytelling.

CASE STUDY – KAIROS TO BUILD BUY-IN FROM THE BOARD

A midsize biopharmaceutical company was preparing to launch its first product. This was the culmination of more than ten years' work, involving a significant and prolonged effort by a large proportion of the company, and it had the full attention of the executive board and investors.

At the same time, the CEO had been working with two senior leaders in the company's discovery department on a new strategy to future-proof the company. This was to involve shifting the discovery engine to a promising but completely new approach to drug discovery, with a restructuring of the R&D departments, and a significant investment to generate a proof of concept.

Formal approval by the company's executive board was crucial.

The original presentation entailed an in-depth scientific discussion of the new approach, including extensive detail on the state-of-the-art research field. It was strong on logos and ethos, weak on pathos. Importantly, it did not create a sense of urgency, or kairos.

They had to turn the final narrative upside down. They started by identifying a big change going on in the company's specific sector – kairos, the opportune moment. The change had been going on for some time but only now were the implications becoming visible. Pipeline opportunities were drying up throughout the sector. As for the pathos, the predicted impact would be dramatic for any company and particularly for their company, which at that time was operating 100% in this changing sector.

How were they taking advantage of this change and future-proofing their company? Their solution lay in embracing a new approach to drug discovery that would massively expand opportunities to identify promising product candidates. This was their new story.

They then presented how they would implement the approach at their company, giving the project a name to make it concrete. All the aspects were clearly grouped into three pillars: the science, the organization, and the manageable risk.

Importantly, key board members were approached individually before the official presentation to discuss with them parts of the idea, thereby creating advance awareness and buy-in.

After a concise and compelling pitch, followed by an extensive discussion, the project was approved unanimously and granted an initial mid-double-digit million-dollar investment to kick-start it.

EXERCISE – THE COLOR OF YOUR STORY

For this exercise, you will need four colored markers, or small sticky notes in four different colors.

- Take your current fundraising pitch deck and print it out.

- Now take the markers or sticky notes and use them to add dots of color based on the four building blocks we discussed earlier in this chapter. Use orange for urgency/kairos, pink for excitement/pathos, blue for credibility/ethos and green for logic/logos. The dots should be big enough to be seen from a distance. For example:

- A slide with lots of scientific data? Green.

- A slide with the incredible achievements of your team? Blue.

- A slide connecting your company to a recent deal that was all over the news? Orange.

- A slide showing a touching story about a patient whose life has been transformed by your solution? Pink.

- You can add multiple dots on each slide, if more than one building block box is ticked. For example, a recent publication in a high-impact journal could get both an orange and a blue dot. Are you showing data from that publication? Add a green dot.

You could even add dots for elements that are not on the slides but are generally part of your pitch. For example, if you open the pitch sharing a strong personal account, add a pink dot on the first slide.

- Now hang the printed pages of the slides on the wall with tape and take a few steps back. Time to look at the final result, the colors on the slides.
- Ask yourself:
  - What is the dominant color you see?
  - What is the least represented color?
  - Is there a color that is missing?
  - Is what you see what you were expecting, based on the stage of your interaction with investors, the audience, and your specific situation?
- Finally, how are you going to use this insight to turn your next pitch into an irresistible story?

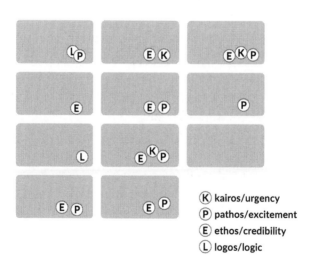

The color of your story

Summary

Understanding how story works is key to take your fundraising game to the next level. We know why investors say no. It's generally because they either don't understand your idea, they don't trust it, they don't get excited by it, or they don't find it urgent or timely.

These four basic elements of compelling communication were identified by Aristotle more than 2000 years ago, and have formed the basis for every successful book, film, or story ever since. They are now the building blocks of the story that you will go on to create.

Your story may take the form of a pitch, but a story is not a pitch. When you're pitching, you're trying to sell something to the audience or get something from them: you want their time, money, and attention. When you're telling a story, you're giving the audience something of great value – an idea that will change their vision of the world for good.

Once you have told your story, it will start spreading exponentially. It will precede you wherever you go. People will line up to hear your story, to get your gift. For the greatest impact, work out the strengths and weaknesses of your pitch. What gift are you giving to the audience?

PART TWO
BUILDING YOUR FUNDRAISING STORY

Now you understand how stories have the power to change your business, and how they work. You also understand why it is so hard to create a compelling story.

It's time for you to build your own fundraising story.

In this section, I'll lead you through the StoryPitch™ model that I use with my clients, which is based on five principles. A winning fundraising story is:

- CEO-driven

- Crystal clear

- Constructed according to classic story structure

- Supported by effective Communication assets
- Aimed at Changing the world

We'll work through each of these points in turn.

FOUR

The CEO Owns The Story

To create a successful story, we need to define who should be doing it. Medium to large companies have a communications department, a business development team, and marketing and sales experts. All these people can contribute to the process and should be encouraged to. In startup companies, the options are often limited to the CEO and the founding team.

But no matter the size of the company and who creates the story, in the end, the *owner* of the story is the CEO. This chapter is about your responsibilities as CEO and how you can carry them out successfully.

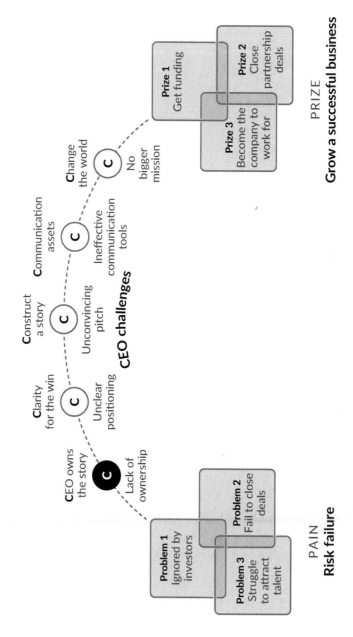

The *StoryPitch™* model

PAIN
Risk failure

Problem 1
Ignored by investors

Problem 2
Fail to close deals

Problem 3
Struggle to attract talent

C CEO owns the story
Lack of ownership

C Clarity for the win
Unclear positioning

C Construct a story
Unconvincing pitch

CEO challenges

C Communication assets
Ineffective communication tools

C Change the world
No bigger mission

PRIZE
Grow a successful business

Prize 1
Get funding

Prize 2
Close partnership deals

Prize 3
Become the company to work for

The company story is the company strategy

As the CEO, it is your responsibility to create a strategy that will guide your company toward success. After all, the CEO is the highest-ranking executive in a company; it is a highly coveted title, and one of the most influential and powerful positions in any organization.

Fundraising puts you and your strategy to the test. Investors don't invest their money in products that are not supported by a compelling strategy. Every meeting, every pitch, every presentation is an opportunity for them to scrutinize it.

As the keeper of the strategy, you are also the keeper of your company story. And it's up to you to make it current and compelling. In the early days of a life sciences startup, when fundraising is especially key, nothing is more crucial than being able to take your science and strategy and weave it into a compelling fundraising narrative that gets investors excited about your vision and your innovation.

In his book, *The Hard Thing About Hard Things*, legendary VC Ben Horowitz reminds us that employees draw from the CEO not only the motivation they need to believe in the big picture, but also meaning for their specific tasks and context for their decisions. This context is more than goals and objectives:

"The story of the company goes beyond quarterly or annual goals and gets to the hard-core question of why."[16]

Employees might ask themselves why they should be excited to work at the company, while investors might ask why they should buy into the product. And for Horowitz, the ultimate question is, "Why is the world better off as a result of this company's existence?" Why is investing in your company a win for the universe as well as for you and for them?

Getting your story straight

The best narratives come from CEOs who take ownership of them.

To live up to your responsibility as keeper of the story, there are five aspects you should prioritize:

1. Starting your company story

2. Assembling the right team

3. Aligning the leadership team around the story

4. Managing negative reactions

5. Getting buy-in from the board

Starting your company story

Like any project, to be successful, the story creation process should have a clear starting moment. Kicking off the process is a crucial step, and the CEO should do that. By initiating it yourself, you send a strong signal to the rest of the organization about how critical it is. This will help you when it comes to making difficult choices and hard decisions later in the process.

Before you make an official communication with your team, take some time to think about the following points:

- Is the timing right? Working on the story will require some effort, in terms of mental energy and time. Make sure you can commit to it.

- Do you have a concrete, important moment coming up when you should have your story ready? Perhaps you are going to meet a prospective partner at a big pharmaceutical company, or you have already been invited to present to some investors, or even at a conference. Having a concrete deadline in mind will help you and the story team focus on delivery.

- What kind of end result would you like to create? Most likely the story will live on several versions of a fundraising pitch deck, but perhaps you want to revamp your website or create a brochure.

Understanding what kind of results you want to generate will help you decide who should join the team and what kind of support you'll need to put in place or hire.

- What will success look like? Imagine yourself in a few weeks' time. You have a clear, compelling story, your investor deck looks awesome, everybody in your leadership team understands it and can deliver the same pitch. Envisioning the end of the process is a powerful way to get you motivated and it will help you to enthuse everybody else.

Assembling the right story team

Creating your fundraising story requires time and effort. But being the owner of the story doesn't mean you have to write it yourself. Assembling the right story team covering all the capacities you need is key to your success.

You need somebody who has a thorough understanding of the science and technology of your product, to make sure your story is solid, built on the best data and anchored in concrete results and science. If you are one of the scientists who founded the company as well as the CEO, you can fill this role, or it might be your co-founder. Usually, though, it is your chief scientific officer or the person in charge of research.

You need the head of business development, who will be pitching the story extensively and probably has a lot of insights into what works and what doesn't work in the current narrative. The rest of the management team should be part of the story team, too, because they have valuable angles to look at the task from.

In my experience, the best and most effective discussions happen in teams of three to four people, including the CEO. Whoever you invite, make sure they understand it is a privilege to be part of the process and that there are expectations that come with it.

Strategy and science are not your only considerations. Dedicated resources will make the process a lot more effective. Scale-up companies often have internal communication support. Their help will be instrumental throughout the project, as you will need access to brand materials as well as support and guidance to create effective messaging for your story.

A presentation designer is a critical support role. Many executives have a personal connection with their pitch deck. They put in many hours perfecting it, fine-tuning the titles of the slides, adding and rearranging content. This can feel satisfying, and PowerPoint is one of the few relatively easy design tools, so you will be tempted to think it's easy to design your presentation yourself. Please resist this temptation, and don't delegate the design to your management team. Having a professional presentation designer take care of the final steps will save you a lot of time, energy, and headaches. The results will be in a different league when produced by an expert.

A copywriter is the second critical support role. After you have drafted the first version of the story, a skilled writer will be instrumental to the project's success. Finding the right words, metaphors, and tone of voice is not easy. Engaging a professional wordsmith will turn your rough diamond of a narrative into a document that will captivate your audience. And it will save you and your team tons of time and frustration.

The leadership team will contribute insights and content and the communications team will help craft the story. If you don't have a communications team – and most startups don't – you could hire an external consultant to bring it together. Often there are other key figures in the organization who need to be involved, for example, those who have specific knowledge about the technology or those who were there before you. Though regardless of who contributes, the final responsibility should remain with you.

Aligning the leadership team around the story

This is perhaps the most important and challenging step. Ask successful investors what they look for in portfolio companies, and many will tell you they'd rather put their money on an average strategy in the hands of a great team than on a great strategy in the hands of an average team.

A story that is not supported by your best people will not go far. How can investors have faith in you if your closest collaborators don't?

Strong leadership teams will have different opinions about individual narrative choices. This can be difficult when the CEO is not the most knowledgeable about the science and technology. It's essential to create a structure where there is room to gain everyone's insight, as well as to make it clear that you as CEO have the last word. There's a fine line between giving freedom and retaining ownership, and you have to manage where that is.

We will explore this further in the next chapter on Clarity.

Managing negative reactions

Expect resistance, and sometimes lots of it, because a new, well-crafted story can be highly polarizing.

This means that while most of your colleagues will love you for it and believe it will help them succeed, others may react defensively and negatively. Perhaps they have been at the company for a long time and they are still committed to the previous narrative.

Perhaps they do not agree on the new strategy, and use critique on the story to channel their frustration.

This is generally a good sign. It means your story is clear, and its clarity is forcing people to make choices. As the CEO and keeper of your company story, it's also your responsibility to get buy-in from your team and create a sense of excitement about where your company is heading.

Here are three tips for handling internal negative feedback on your new story.

Wait: Take time to process your emotions. It's easy to have an emotional reaction when hearing negative comments. If you get irritated or defensive, take a deep breath, remain calm, and keep your feelings in check.

Acknowledge: Change is hard for anyone. Be grateful for the feedback, and mention that you understand the emotional and practical implications of the points mentioned. Openly acknowledging the reaction is an important step to move on.

Respond: Be clear that this is not just a presentation; this is the company strategy, and the strategy does not change every day. But it is not cast in stone either. Over the course of the next months, you will be observing how your investors, peers, and potential partners react to it, then adjusting it where needed.

Getting buy-in from the board

Most CEOs can rely on advisers or a formal board of directors to provide guidance and advice on their leadership. These board members certainly need to be involved in the story. As the company story is a manifestation of its strategy, the board needs to be informed and be given a formal role in the process. Remember also that the way you interact with your board members informs how they think of you as a leader, manager, and strategist.

When is the right time to tell the board members? Generally, they do not have time to be involved with the creation of the story, but they do want to be part of the process. The best moments are at the beginning and at the end. Let your board know that you are about to start the process of creating a new or revised company story and that you will share a draft with them when it is ready. You might want to have a conversation with one or two trusted board members to hear directly from them what they think about the current narrative, possible criticisms, or ideas to strengthen it.

A good time to present the story to the board is when you have a solid draft pitch deck. In many cases, the story is circulated internally as a deck and feedback is gathered from each member. Although commonplace and convenient, this method is not ideal. I have personally seen many great stories killed because of misinterpretations or limited grasp of the intended narrative based on the slides – which is a painful situation at this late stage of the process.

A much better way to go about things is to make time for the presentation during a board meeting. Make sure the board understands the importance of this step. It's not about reviewing slides together, which would not be a good use of their time. You are giving them the privilege of hearing the new strategic narrative of your company, which will be the basis for the next fundraising round, deal-making, recruiting, and so on.

If a presentation is not an option, a good alternative is to share the script of the story, including a few slides as figures to illustrate key points and to satisfy their appetite for visuals.

If for whatever reason you have to share the whole deck in advance of formally presenting it, make sure you manage the board's expectations. Be clear about what they are going to review. Is this a teaser deck or a full company deck? Help them understand how they should look at the document they receive from you. Also, the deck, document, or whatever you want them to read needs to be in their inboxes three to five business days before the board meeting. Don't fire decks off at the last minute with the excuse that you were waiting for final figures or slides to be added.

No matter how many people worked on the story with you, make sure it is you who presents it to the board. That will send the right signal that you own the story and that it's not some sort of marketing product. Sometimes it can be useful to have somebody from your management team present part of story, perhaps to cover the science content. They will value the exposure to the board, and the board will get a chance to see how the story has been internalized by the team, as opposed to being your brainchild that still needs to gain support internally.

The board's feedback can take many forms. Some members might talk about a general impression, others might go into depth on the narrative and the slides. They will provide valuable insights on gaps, inconsistencies, and weaknesses in the story and their feedback is vital to make it watertight. Often your investors sit on the board and their support is particularly important, as they can be valuable ambassadors for your story.

Of course, incorporating too many conflicting ideas is a sure recipe for failure. You will not need to take on every element of the board's feedback. You'll need to maintain a fine balance here, and it will require all your ability to manage sensitivities, but in the end, you should only incorporate feedback that you feel adds value to the story.

In any case, make sure to let the board know that their feedback has been taken seriously. Tell them how you incorporated their suggestions and share the final product with them.

CASE STUDY – THE CEO AS THE STORY CHAMPION

A biotechnology startup focused on discovering and developing innovative therapies for the treatment of severe ophthalmology diseases was preparing to raise funding. As the spin-off of a renowned European research institute, it had secured enough funding for the initial proof-of-concept studies. Now it needed substantial capital to bring the lead compound to the clinic.

The feedback the CEO was getting from investors and advisers was lukewarm. Interesting technology, but hard to make sense of its relevance. Complexity was in the way: complex science, complex slides, complex pitch. Scientific results and financial projections dominated the slides. Besides that, the story was primarily centered on the company. Audiences were not getting excited.

To create a winning fundraising narrative, the CEO turned the focus of the story and introduced the patient's perspective – literally, by showing slides as visually impaired patients would see them, ie, mostly black, with a tiny light spot in the middle.

The CEO also created a clear narrative that explained the tragedy of the disease and the business opportunity without immediately diving into the complexity of the science.

Finally, instead of a fundraising pitch asking for money, the CEO positioned the company as the champions of patients and their families, offering investors an opportunity to change the lives of so many sufferers.

Armed with the new fundraising story, the CEO won a prestigious pitch competition, was awarded initial multimillion-dollar funding from a leading

European agency, and a few months later, secured an oversubscribed mid-double-digit million-dollar Series A.

EXERCISE – WRITE YOUR COMPANY'S OBITUARY

Imagine that your company is a person who, many years from now, has passed away. What would you want to be written about it?

- Spend fifteen to twenty minutes writing down whatever words, phrases, and sentences come to mind.

- Don't overthink or censor yourself; don't analyze or critique your thoughts.

- Don't worry about giving perfect answers. You can revisit this exercise in the future.

- Some questions you could ask yourself as you do this exercise are:

    What did my company do?

    What change did it bring about?

    What impact did it have?

    What core character traits and values did my company staff consistently demonstrate throughout their working life?

    Who was part of my company?

    Who did my company care for?

    How did my company impact or change these people?

    What were the major accomplishments of my company?

    What was my company passionate about?

What was my company legacy?

- Remember, it's just an exercise. Think big, imagine possibilities. Recall inspiring dreams and thoughts you've had in the past and share them with your colleagues. Even better, read your obituaries out loud to one another.

You'll be surprised.

Summary

No matter what the size of your company, and who contributes to the story, the owner of the story is the CEO. By improving the story, you improve the strategy. Not surprisingly, the most compelling narratives come from CEOs who take ownership of them.

But that doesn't mean the CEO can or should create the story alone. You need a team of people that support you in the process, both internally and externally.

It's important to align your leadership team around your story. It's essential to create a structure where there is room to gain everyone's insight, as well as to make clear that you still have the last word.

Finally, you need to be able to share your story with the board, manage the feedback process and make sure the board knows you take their feedback seriously.

FIVE
Clarity For The Win

We live in a world where information is cheap and abundant. Before you start creating more information, it's worth investing time in understanding the world your company is operating in. Only with complete clarity about the context can we understand the value of our big idea, product, and company.

Rather than focusing on yourself, look outside your office. What is happening in the world right now? What is troubling your audience?

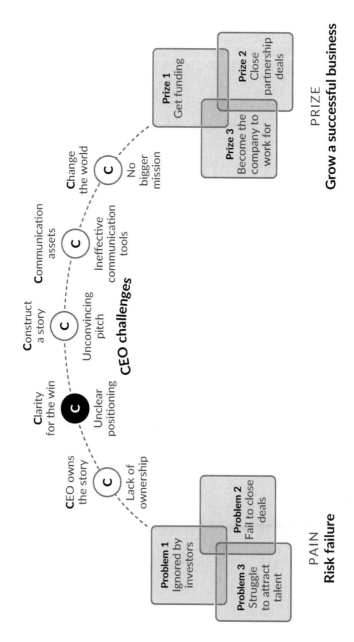

The StoryPitch™ model

CEO challenges

CEO owns the story — Lack of ownership

Clarity for the win — Unclear positioning

Construct a story — Unconvincing pitch

Communication assets — Ineffective communication tools

Change the world — No bigger mission

PAIN
Risk failure

Problem 1 Ignored by investors

Problem 2 Fail to close deals

Problem 3 Struggle to attract talent

PRIZE
Grow a successful business

Prize 1 Get funding

Prize 2 Close partnership deals

Prize 3 Become the company to work for

Clear timing, or "Why now?"

The clarity that you most need is about timing: why the moment is right for you. When professional screenwriters pitch their scripts, they know that's the first question they need to answer. That's because they know their story – like your science, your product, and your company – doesn't exist in a vacuum.

Context matters, more than any other factor. Nobody can say with absolute certainty what will succeed and what will fail, but if we look at what has worked in the past, we can connect the dots. It's not always the first to market that succeeds.

MySpace had all the makings to be a killer, norm-shattering innovation, but it was Facebook that soared. AltaVista had every chance of being the world's favorite search engine, but it was Google that claimed the title.

"Why now?" Why was the world more ready for Facebook than for MySpace a few years earlier? Why did we greet Google with open arms, when AltaVista had already brought us the same technology?

And in the life sciences sector, why did nearly every vaccine company that considered working on mRNA in the 2000s decide to invest its resources elsewhere, whereas BioNTech was catapulted into the limelight as a global pioneer in the COVID-19 race to vaccine development and emerged as one of the pandemic's greatest success stories?

Back to Aristotle's ancient Greek building blocks and his kairos. Those tech innovations and their stories took off when they did because we were finally in a place to hear them. As Marc Andreessen of a16z tells us, "There are no bad ideas in tech – only bad timing."[17]

Trends are a powerful opportunity. Nobody would ever call a global pandemic fortuitous. But ask any storyteller and they'll tell you tragedy generates inspiration.

It's only when we're confronted with crisis that we see the gaps of our own ways of living. The 2020 COVID pandemic, for instance, brought about novel technologies, heightened procedures, and accelerated regulatory protocols to an audience that was ready to welcome them (or quickly became ready, because we needed all those things). The context for these technological innovations wasn't just obvious, but urgent. And where there's urgency, there's resounding impact.

Urgency first

Crises are exemplary drivers of innovation because they make it easy for investors to visualize the impact of the technology and hear the ticking clock behind them.

But not every pitch has to be connected to pandemics, social uprisings, or global issues. You can find just as much urgency in the smaller stuff: a new position paper by the Food and Drug Administration, perhaps, or a key opinion leader calling for solutions just like yours.

The common thread is change. When you ground your pitch in a world that you can show us is changing, you're bringing urgency into the ring. Your audience can choose to bite or be left behind – and that's something that'll weigh on them far beyond the boardroom.

Like Hollywood producers, Sequoia Capital knows that the most effective way to pitch an idea is to start it off by answering, "Why now?" In their guide to presenting to investors, they advise you to answer "What's changed? Explain what's the discontinuous shift, break-through, or innovation that opens the window to create a substantial new company."[18]

Every founder who makes it into the room to pitch has a good idea. It's your job to show your audience that you have a good idea and to convince them that right now is the right time, the kairos, for it to flourish.

Raise the stakes. Apply the urgency. Help your audience feel the impact. With timing in your corner, you can do it.

Clear positioning, or framing

The ability to frame ideas in a compelling manner is critical for companies working on innovation. Developing new products involves enormous levels of uncertainty. Entrepreneurs need to get their story straight if they want to attract attention and funding. So, what is the most effective way for a company to frame its innovation pitch?

The winds of change

Based on the analysis of over a thousand cases, experts at McKinsey studied the categories into which business stories tend to fall and how these categories impact their success. They discovered that nearly half of most of the successful cases were those that rode big global trends.[19] The successful entrepreneurs positioned themselves as expert navigators who caught the wind of change and were in the right place at the right time. They did so not by sheer luck, but thanks to a powerful blend of experience, instinct, and vision that placed the CEO, the management team, and the company in a unique position relative to their competitors.

Things will never be the same

This "big change" approach is also the starting point advocated by strategic messaging and positioning expert Andy Raskin, who argues that "great pitches start with change." By identifying and responding to an undeniable shift in the world, entrepreneurs can create both big stakes and tremendous urgency for their proposition. When the world is changing, no one wants to be left behind.[20]

This change should not be debatable, but something new and, at the same time, already visible. Because the entrepreneurs are part of a significant, observable global shift, their ideas are more likely to succeed. Your product or innovation helps prospects embrace and thrive in the new world that the change is creating.

Go global

But what kinds of major shifts are useful to frame an innovation story? McKinsey has identified three hot spaces in which innovation "temperature" is high: global growth shifts, new societal deals, and accelerating industry disruption.[21]

Investors love companies that respond to these unstoppable trends. And a company benefiting from such tailwinds is much more likely to rise to the top of the economic-profit performance charts than one that is facing headwinds.

A ride into the future

As renowned screenwriting lecturer Robert McKee puts it in his book, *Story: Substance, structure, style and the principles of screenwriting*, change is what grabs people's attention, and great stories are all about how and why life changes in response to an irreversible event.[22] As long as things are moving on an even keel, you pay attention to whatever you're doing. But if something around you changes – if the temperature around you drops, if the phone rings – that draws your attention.

Business leaders who understand the changes underway and who are able to convert them into a compelling strategic narrative have an extraordinary opportunity to make an impact. When they pitch their company, they are not asking investors to fund a promising business with a ground-breaking product. Instead, they are offering investors the opportunity to be part of a revolution, a new way of thinking, living, and working. They are selling them a ticket to the future.

Clear problem, or the three dimensions of the problem

Every problem has three dimensions. And it is important to address all three dimensions if you want to make an impact with your audience.

The three dimensions of the problem

The first dimension is the practical, objective problem you're solving. This is the easiest dimension to talk about. Perhaps you have developed a new drug that can stop a pathway of aging, or a new vaccine that elicits a high immune response against an incurable disease. It's usually easy to describe the practical problem because it's based on facts and data. It's what your science and technology address.

But as we have discussed, people do not take important decisions based only on logic and facts and data and rationality. We make choices based on emotions. We call this our "gut feeling." And it's only after we get this gut feeling that we use data and logic and facts and science to justify our decision. This is also true for investors.

This is where the personal dimension of the problem comes in. It is an essential component of decision-making. What makes your pitch so appealing to the audience? Perhaps they just missed an important deal to competitor VCs. Or they faced a big setback in their development pipeline. Or a competitor just published important results that put them in a weak position.

Then there is a third dimension of the problem, which is on a bigger scale: the philosophical problem, the existential problem, the global problem that your company, science, and product is addressing. Perhaps you have developed a technology or a drug solution that might turn into a cure for cancer one day. Or perhaps you have developed a platform that makes vaccine production possible anywhere in the world, even in developing countries that do not have current access to vaccines. Perhaps you want to get rid of a certain disease altogether.

This is the bigger problem you're solving. This is your ambitious goal, your vision for the future.

Could it be your technology that will rid the world of cancer, or infectious diseases, or Alzheimer's? Perhaps, one day. And if that could happen, your audience wants to be part of the story.

Make sure your philosophical problem feels relevant to the practical problem you are solving. Investors see CEOs claiming they want to cure cancer or Alzheimer's every day. Perhaps you are focusing on a particular aspect of developing the cure, like making a promising therapeutic approach available to a large number of patients, or ensuring patients do not relapse after an initial successful therapy.

When you address a clear and logically defined practical problem, combined with a mission, a vision, a big ambition, and you combine it with the personal struggle or the emotional problem of your audience, that's where the magic happens. That's where you get the audience excited about your pitch.

Using the audience's personal problem also allows you to fine-tune your pitch to tell your story to many different audiences without having to change the narrative. You could be talking to a large healthcare organization like a hospital, or a senior leader at a pharmaceutical company, so you need to be able to adapt your presentation to the audience. Adjusting the personal problem is the best way to construct stories that are specific to different audiences, without changing the overall structure. You can't change the practical problem because you can't change your solution, and you don't want to change your philosophical ambition too often, or you will seem inconsistent. So, focus on changing the emotional problem.

CASE STUDY - KAIROS TO CREATE URGENCY

A group of seasoned industry leaders and world-class scientists had banded together to fight an untreatable viral disease with a new approach. Their technology was based on deep and complex science and grounded on evidence extrapolated from other studies. But there was no hard data yet, let alone a proof-of-concept study. Additionally, given the ongoing global emergency, they had to compete for the attention of investors with many other companies working on different technologies in the same area.

Instead of pitching a technology narrative, the founders decided to focus their story on the novelty of the approach. Not just better science, but a new vision for a future in which we would approach this threat differently.

They anchored their vision to a global shift in people's attitudes towards self-medication, a megatrend already happening and destined to change healthcare for good.

By proving they were part of this movement, they were able to create an inspiring fundraising story that got the attention of world-class VCs and secured mid-double-digit million-dollar Series A funding.

Clear communication, or the elephant in the room

On 18 September 2007, Carnegie Mellon professor Randy Pausch was asked to deliver a "Last Lecture." This was a tradition at Carnegie Mellon University, something that many colleagues had done before him, an opportunity to talk about what wisdom they would impart to the world if they knew it was their last chance.

As Pausch took center stage in front of hundreds of people, he seemed nervous, cracked a few jokes. Then he told the audience that his dad always taught him, "When there's an elephant in the room, introduce it." So he did, "in case there is anybody who just wandered in and doesn't know the backstory."

Pausch told the crowd he had terminal cancer, then showed them an image of the tumor in his liver. The slide was titled, "The Elephant in the Room." He told the audience that there was no hope, nothing could get rid of the tumor.

The video of his moving speech has been viewed more than 20 million times,[23] and the book version was on *The New York Times* best-seller list for more than 100 weeks.[24]

CEOs pitching to VCs often struggle with their version of the elephant in the room. Maybe your elephant looks a bit like this:

- You're pitching, but you're not the CEO.

- Your famous co-founder has just posted on social that she's leaving the company.

- A direct competitor of your pre-clinical product has just announced the successful completion of a Phase 2 clinical trial.

- You're operating in a notoriously oversaturated market.

- Many others have already tried your approach and failed.

As you're presenting, investors will be able to tell there is a problem. They might not be able to work out exactly what it is, and maybe, either for legal reasons or simply because they're too polite, they won't ask. On the other hand, they might already know what it is and notice that you're not talking about it.

There's only one way to deal with your elephant, and that's head-on. Face up to your elephant. Rather than pretend it isn't in the room, introduce it early in your presentation. If VCs have to ask about your elephant first, it will feel like they're "catching you out." But if you bring it up, it's no longer such an issue.

INSIDE STORY - ARE YOU THE PROBLEM?

This may be hard to take. But sometimes you yourself are the elephant in the room, the reason why you did not get the outcome you wanted. Maybe you didn't get funding simply because investors didn't feel there was a strong enough connection there.

Were you able to convince them that you are a good fit for the market? That you have the skills, experience, and network to make your startup a success? How were your interactions with your co-founder and the rest of the team? Did you come across as a stellar group of complementary talents? Poor team dynamics can strongly deter investors.

And the hardest reason of all to hear? They might have felt that you're not honest. Your presentation may have been perceived as lacking objective evidence and being overly subjective, causing your audience to doubt your honesty and integrity.

If you have the feeling you are part of the problem, try to understand what triggered that reaction. If you can, ask for feedback, preferably one to one. If that is not possible, you could reach out to a trusted adviser who has seen you pitch before. And always ask your team for their honest opinion. You might be surprised by what they have to tell you.

Do you have an elephant in the room? The answer is always yes – but it may not be the one you think. Before you go into any presentation and introduce a potential elephant, do a quick reality check with one or two people you trust to find out if they are seeing the same elephant as you.

One giant elephant that we are all staring at is the global pandemic. Rather than skim over it, talk honestly about how COVID-19 has impacted your business – for better or worse. You can build a section into your slide deck or talk it through, whatever works best for you. Just don't pretend it isn't there.

Remember Randy Pausch. He said, "We cannot change the cards we are dealt, just how we play the hand."

What's your elephant in the room? And when are you going to tell us about it?

Summary

Good pitches start with a problem or a product or a team. Great pitches start with change.

By identifying and responding to an undeniable shift in the world, you can convey a sense of high stakes and pressing urgency to your audience. When the world is changing, no one wants to be left behind.

Your job is to help investors understand why the right time for your product is now and to explain clearly the significant shift, breakthrough, or innovation that has opened the field to a substantial new player – your company.

Studies have shown that successful entrepreneurs position themselves as expert navigators of the winds of change, being in the right place at the right time. But that change should not be something debatable. It should be visible. Business leaders who understand the change and can build it into a compelling narrative have an extraordinary opportunity to make an impact.

Identify the problem that your company is really solving. Problems have three distinct dimensions: the practical/objective problem, the personal/emotional problem perceived by your audience, and the wider philosophical problem. To convince your audience, you need to address all three.

And don't forget to understand your elephant in the room and what it means for you. What is the one thing that investors are thinking about during your pitch that they might not be asking you about, either out of courtesy, or because they think it will be too embarrassing? We all have an elephant in the room but sometimes it's not the one we think. Face up to yours and talk about it, before the audience does.

SIX
Construct A Story

You now have a clear idea of the problems you are solving and the position of your big idea in the world. It's time to start constructing your story.

A solid story needs a solid foundation. All the greatest stories ever told, all the best books ever written, all the blockbuster movies ever made share the same recurring elements. First, they revolve about a change, big or small, that creates a problem, a challenge, an opportunity. Second, they follow the same structure to introduce and organize the information. And third, they have a hero, whose responsibility it ultimately is to fix the problem.

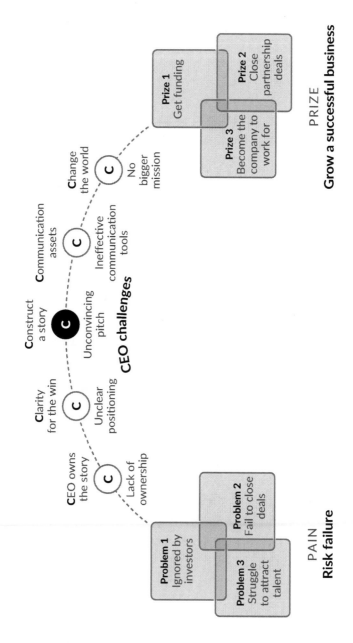

The StoryPitch™ model

The three-act structure

Whether you're writing a book, the screenplay for a movie, or the story of a company, you have many options for organizing your material. But there is one structure that is most commonly used in all forms of storytelling, and has been since the first stories were told. We refer to it as the three-act structure.

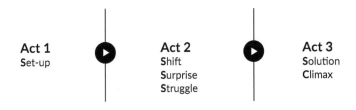

Act 1	Act 2	Act 3
Set-up	Shift	Solution
	Surprise	Climax
	Struggle	

The three-act structure

Act 1 of the story is typically the **set-up**. This refers to the introduction of the characters and the framing of the narrative, before anything important happens.

Act 2, the middle part, opens with a turning point. There is a sudden **shift**, something happens – something surprising, unexpected, sometimes dramatic. And that changes the energy of the story and forces our hero to go into action. In good movies, we're really interested in this shift and the ensuing struggle of the hero, so most of the story takes place in the second act.

Act 3 is about the **solution** to the struggle, the resolution of the situation. The hero confronts the problem, may or may not solve it, and gains important insights on the way to the final resolution. And we, the audience, gain the same insights. We are changed.

In a fundraising story, Act 1 is about setting the narrative. Keep this section simple. You want the audience to acknowledge this early information. You want heads nodding. You don't want the audience to get confused and start asking questions or seeing a problem before you even get to the action.

Act 2 is where you want to surprise your audience. This is where you can make a real difference in how your pitch is received, by coming up with something your audience didn't know or didn't realize. It does not always have to be presented as a problem – it can be a surprising revelation, a new interpretation of existing data, or a change happening in the sector.

The third and final act, named the solution, brings the audience a new idea or understanding. Remember, this new insight should not be about your product, but instead a general piece of wisdom or intelligence which becomes the theme of the story. If the audience learns nothing new in this section and nothing happened for them, then it's not a story. After establishing this theme, at the climax of the story, you can offer your solution – what you are selling

In a three-act structure, your fundraising story would sound something like this:

Act 1: Set-up

We all know that…
Studies have shown that…

Act 2: Surprise, shift, struggle

Unfortunately, few people realize that…
Unexpectedly, recent results have proven that…

Act 3: Solution, climax

We need to…
The only way to overcome this problem is…

Your solution

We have a developed a product that does just that…
Our technology addresses exactly this…
Let me show you how it works…

A story is not a scientific paper

The three-act story structure may look like the structure we follow when writing or talking about science in a publication or presentation. Introduction, results, discussion. Sound familiar? The similarity, though, is only on the surface.

In a scientific publication, the introduction can be lengthy and complicated, as it is meant to bring the audience to the same level of knowledge as the author. Without that knowledge, your peers will not be able to understand and appreciate what is coming next, your new unique findings. The introduction to a paper mentions many previous publications and provides an overview of results obtained so far. It sets out the current preoccupations, challenges, and insights related to your sector to provide context. There is a lot of scientific background information with very little space for action.

In many scientific presentations at conferences or events, too, the effect is of one big introduction. This is how we are used to operating. When we talk about science, we apply the same structure that we use when we write about it. We come at it from the same mental space. But to tell our fundraising story, we need to make adjustments.

The story is not a scientific publication, far from it. In a good story, the set-up is simple and uncomplicated. It's only the framing of your narrative, the introduction of the main stakeholders and the situation. When you say, "We all know that...", you want to see heads nodding.

In a three-act fundraising story, the surprises happen in Act 2. In a blockbuster movie, the surprise or the struggle generally occupies most of the story in one breath-taking action scene after another. There is very little introduction. Let's see what else we can learn from films.

Examples from the movies: The three-act structure

The three-act structure is used in most Hollywood movies, because it's something we all have learned to recognize as the structure of a great story, even if we are only subconsciously aware of it. Let's consider how it works in one of my favorite movies, *Jaws*.[25]

Act 1: Set-up

Amity Island, a small community whose main business asset is its beaches, is preparing for the upcoming Independence Day weekend, the most profitable time of the year. We meet the new sheriff, Martin Brody. He has moved with his family from New York City hoping for a more relaxed and safer life.

Act 2: Surprise, shift, struggle

One day, a great white shark decides to make the small resort town of Amity his private feeding grounds. Several people are killed before Sheriff Brody manages to close the beaches to swimmers and to hire a local fisherman, Quint, who is an experienced shark hunter.

Act 3: Solution, climax

As the shark hunter's boat is sinking and all seems lost, Brody tosses a scuba tank into the shark's mouth and fires his rifle at it, blowing the shark to smithereens.

Did you remember the ending? Often, we might forget how a movie ends, even in our favorite movies. It's because the end is not the most important part. What we really love in good stories is the struggle.

If you know how to use this three-act structure, you can tell your story in thirty seconds, as I did in the short summary of *Jaws*, when you meet an investor briefly at an event. Or in thirty minutes, when you are invited to give a keynote presentation. Or in three hours, when you have the time to tell the whole tale, such as during an in-depth meeting with investors who are interested in hearing more. But you're always telling the same story, whatever its length.

Share a big idea, don't sell your product

All great stories, whether they are movies, novels, or children's fairy tales, are about a bigger idea than the plot unfolded in the narrative.

For instance, "Little Red Riding Hood" is not just a story about a little girl who encounters a big bad wolf in the forest. There is the bigger idea that the story conveys, which is that the world is a dangerous place and children should listen to their parents or something bad will happen to them.

The big idea behind *Jaws* is that, despite the progress of human civilization, we're not invincible and nature is still sometimes our enemy. The ocean is a dangerous place. And when danger materializes, we have to fight it with everything we have, as we have done since time immemorial in the age-old tale of man versus beast.

When Elon Musk pitched his Tesla Powerwall, he did not go on stage to sell better rechargeable batteries. He was there to share the big idea that we are on course to destroying our planet with our addiction to fossil fuels. Should we do something about it? Of course we should, and solar energy may well be the solution to our pollution problem.

The hero

Once you have created a clear structure, it's time to introduce the hero. This is the character who is going to solve the problem. Deciding who should be the hero of your story is a fundamental decision for the success of your pitch.

Take *Kill Bill*, another one of my favorite movies.[26] The hero of the movie is Uma Thurman's character, a former assassin known as The Bride. She wakes up from a coma after her jealous ex-lover Bill has tried to murder her on her wedding day. She vows to get even with every person who contributed to the loss of her unborn child, her entire wedding party, and four years of her life. Bill has caused a lot of pain and she is going to fix this by killing him.

Whenever I watch *Kill Bill*, I get very excited. I feel as if I am fighting Bill myself. And that's exactly how a good action movie should make us feel. We, the audience, identify with the hero. We feel we are the hero of the movie, participating in a big adventure without even leaving our seats. And the feeling stays long after we leave the movie theater, due to the hormones that were released during the storytelling.

That's what you should be trying to achieve with your pitch, your presentation, your fundraising story. It's your responsibility to make the audience feel they're the hero, because they are the ones who are going to solve the problem. Not you, not your product, not your company. The audience will solve the problem, by investing in your company, by licensing your technology, by buying your products.

What's your superpower?

Have you noticed? Heroes are often reluctant to answer the call to action. They don't want to be heroes. They have their own life, why should they risk everything to solve a huge problem?

As such, heroes need a little help to get into action. In movies, this critical help often comes in the form of a superpower, a special weapon or tool. Heroes need this superpower to feel they stand a chance of winning. They need this to answer the call to action and solve the problem.

Your role is to provide the superpower. In your fundraising story, this is your product. You are not the hero but the one who provides the superpower for the hero, the audience, to use.

Examples from the movies: The hero's superpower

This concept of superpower for the hero is something that comes back in many movies. In *Kill Bill*, it's a weapon.

Does The Bride initially want to kill Bill and his assassins? Of course not. She used to be in love with Bill. And she's trying to build a new life. She is preparing to get married, to have a baby, to have a regular happy life with her family. Even after she decides to kill Bill, she knows it's going to be tough. It's quite possible that Bill or one of his gang members will kill her.

To stand a chance against them, she needs a special weapon, a sword made by the best sword maker in the world. The strongest, sharpest, and deadliest samurai sword ever made. Armed with this sword, her new superpower, The Bride will be able to eliminate all Bill's assassins one-by-one and, in the end, kill Bill – although not with the sword.

Sometimes the superpower is not a special weapon but a special ability. In *The Incredible Hulk*, a shy researcher turns into a giant green monster with superhuman strength and speed.[27] And some other times the super-power is something humbler, like the pair of skates in *Whip It*, which gives the free-spirited teenager Bliss an escape route from the career in beauty pageants her mother has planned for her.[28]

Examples from ancient Greece: Odysseus's bow

This concept of a superpower for the hero is of course not new. Heroes have had their special superpowers since antiquity. Homer's *Odyssey*, an ancient Greek epic poem and one of the oldest works of literature, gives us one such example.[29] It covers the ten years that it takes Odysseus to return to his home, Ithaca, from Troy, where he had already spent ten years fighting.

Back in Ithaca, his wife Penelope is having difficulties. She does not know whether Odysseus is alive or dead. In his absence, she is being besieged by men who want to marry her and gain possession of the kingdom.

Odysseus arrives home after all his trials, disguised as a beggar. Penelope sets up a bowstringing and archery contest with Odysseus's bow. One after another, Penelope's suitors try and fail to string the bow. But then Odysseus strings the bow, lines up twelve axe handles and shoots an arrow through all of them. He then goes on to slaughter Penelope's suitors.

Does Odysseus want to kill the suitors? Of course not. He is an old man. He's tired of fighting. He wants to be home with his wife and son. He needs a special tool, a superhuman power to give him the strength he needs. In this case, it's his own bow, which was at home waiting for him.

Organizing your data

Once you have introduced the big idea, it's time to take a deep dive into the technology of your product and the strategy of your business. You probably have a vast amount of data and information to organize.

Science, financials, market analysis, and much more. How should you tackle it?

It's time to apply logic. Let's take a look.

Choose the right logic

Scientists are used to applying what is called deductive logic. We start from a statement, a premise we know to be true. We then make an observation and draw a conclusion based on that observation.

For example, we know that transcription factors activate genes. We observed in the lab that the A1 protein activates the X1 gene. From this observation, we deduce that the A1 protein is a transcription factor. We can repeat this for all the proteins belonging to the A family and if they all activate one of the X genes, we can conclude that A proteins are a family of transcription factors.

If you have a science background, this will sound familiar to you. This is how the scientific method works. It's critical for doing science, but it's not the best way to talk about science.

The problem with the deductive approach is that you create a long string of information, data, and observations arranged linearly. It takes forever to make your main point and it's almost impossible to summarize or shorten the observations, because you would interrupt the sequence. That makes for a long and winding story.

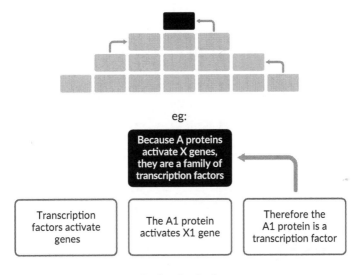

eg:

Because A proteins activate X genes, they are a family of transcription factors

Transcription factors activate genes

The A1 protein activates X1 gene

Therefore the A1 protein is a transcription factor

Deductive logic

You can't change the science, so try changing the logic. Rather than deductive logic, use inductive logic, which starts with the conclusion, or the big idea, and links it to the supporting evidence.

Let's revisit the example above using inductive logic. The conclusion now becomes the opening: A proteins are a family of transcription factors. Then we present the evidence supporting the idea. To identify this, ask, "How can you say that?"

In this case, the answers are "because they activate X genes," "because they bind to DNA," and "because they have an activation domain."

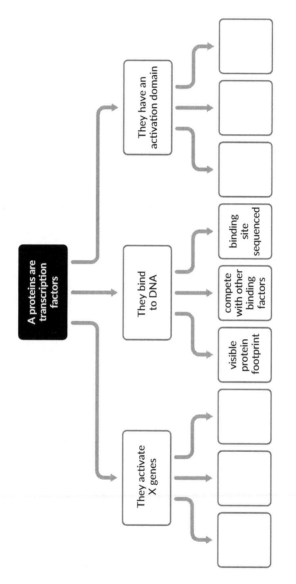

Inductive logic

For each statement you can go deeper. Ask again, "How can you say that?" and mention the supporting evidence. For example, you can say, "they bind to DNA" because they have a visible protein footprint, they compete with other DNA binding factors, and they have a DNA binding domain.

By continuing in this way, you organize your information vertically in pillars to form a pyramid. Depending on the audience, you can decide how deep you want to go in this pyramid, or which elements of the pyramid you wish to draw attention to. But the structure of your story does not need to change.

INSIDE STORY - CURE VERSUS PREVENTION

Selling the cure is always easier than selling the prevention. It's human nature.

If we are heading to the beach and want to lose weight, we are willing to pay for an expensive pill, diet, or personal trainer to get fast results. We are not so interested in a daily healthy lifestyle with long-term benefits.

It's also why cancer drugs can command a high price, whereas vaccination rates in the western world are declining.

But when the risk of catching a deadly virus gets dangerously close, prevention feels like a cure. The spread of the COVID-19 virus has created urgency.

If your product is inherently preventive, creating urgency will help you position it as a cure and get your audience's undivided attention.

The power of three

Things that come in threes are easier to remember and make an impact:

- Veni, vidi, vici

- Liberté, égalité, fraternité

- Location, location, location

- Small, medium, large

- The Good, the Bad and the Ugly

In rhetoric, this is called the tricolon, a series of three parallel words, verbs, or phrases that stress three important points. Tricolons are one of the most powerful rhetorical devices. They help the reader absorb the idea and remember it more effectively.

There is nothing magical about the number three. It works because it is based on the way our brains process information. Recognizing patterns is an essential part of how humans make decisions – it helps us make sense of all the information we are exposed to constantly. Three just happens to be the smallest number of elements required to create a pattern. Studies have also shown the optimal number of positive claims is three.[30]

Use the power of three to your advantage when telling your story by organizing all your information into a three-pillar structure. By doing this, you can present a lot of complex content, such as a large body of scientific evidence or your clinical results, into a form that is easy for you to convey and for your audience to remember.

For instance, when you present your product in your pitch you could summarize it into the following three claims: it's effective, it's safe, and it's scalable.

For "it's effective," you could show the *in vitro* and *in vivo* data, and perhaps results from clinical trials.

"It's safe" would cover the results on specificity, or biodegradability, or the lack of side effects.

Finally, the third pillar, "It's scalable" allows you to showcase how you can manufacture your product at a scale that makes it clinically and economically interesting.

So you might say something like: "This is exactly what we are doing at our company. We have created a product that does just that. It's effective [1], it's safe [2], and it's scalable [3]. Let me show you how it works."

If you don't have time to show the results, people will still remember the three pillars.

EXERCISE: THE THREE PILLARS OF YOUR PRESENTATION

- Print out all your presentation slides, lay them out on a table or stick them on a wall.
- Identify the key message of each slide in a short sentence and write the sentence on a sticky note.
- As you write each slide's message, remove the slide from its place on the wall (or table) and put the sticky note summary in its place.
- Continue until you have replaced all the slides with sticky notes.
- Look carefully at the display. You will likely find that some of the notes express similar or related messages. Group these together until you end up with clusters of related messages.
- Ideally have three clusters. If you have more, merge some into a larger cluster.
- Use these clusters or "pillars" to create the three-pillar structure for your presentation.

Summary

To stand the test of time, a story needs a solid foundation and a consistent structure.

The three-act structure has endured for millennia. It is used in most successful movies and books because it works.

Act 1 delivers the set-up and introduces the characters and world of the story. In a fundraising story, this is simple and straightforward, giving information that your investors will find easy to process.

Act 2 opens with a surprise, a shift leading to the story's main action with all its complications and struggles. In your pitch, the aim here is to deliver something your audience doesn't know, or is not aware of, such as a new insight to persuade them that the time to act or invest is now.

Act 3 delivers the solution to the predicament of Act 2. This should not be about your product, but a general approach – a high-level solution. You should highlight your story's theme and give the audience a bigger-picture understanding before asking for anything from them. Then, at the climax of Act 3, you can offer your solution.

Scientific publications and presentations seem to have a three-act structure (introduction, results, and discussion), but the similarity is only at the surface. They have a top-heavy first act laden with necessary background information, which we have to adjust if we want to tell our fundraising story.

Like any great story, your fundraising journey needs a hero – but it shouldn't be you. You should treat your audience as the hero, take them on the hero's journey and give them the gift of your big idea before you ask for them to take action. The audience should be drawn into your story as though they are living the hero's experience.

When it's time to offer your solution, you will have a lot of scientific data to organize. Traditionally, scientists use deductive logic. We start from a premise, make an observation, and draw a conclusion. This results in a huge sequence of data and observations, with the conclusion far away at the end. This is hard for your audience to absorb, so you need to shift to inductive logic, where you start at the top of the pyramid with the conclusion and decide how much supporting data it is appropriate to provide for your particular audience.

The power of three is another enduring rule of story structure, with roots in the ancient art of rhetoric and cognitive science. By organizing your information into three major pillars or claims, you can help the audience understand and be convinced by your story.

SEVEN

Create Communication Assets

Now that you have constructed a compelling story that clarifies your strategy and will tell your audience about your big idea, you need to create effective communication assets to help you share the story with investors – and the world.

Why you need communication assets

A drawing on a piece of paper is not a painting. The plot for a novel that has never been written is not a Pulitzer-winning book. A script that remains unspoken is never going to be a blockbuster movie. A story needs support to be spread widely. It's not enough to have it in your head or on some printed sheets.

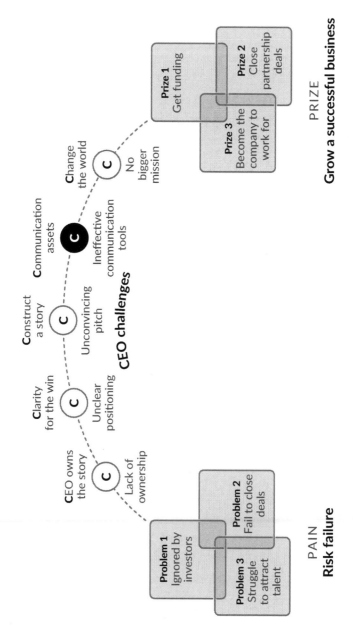

The StoryPitch™ model

All of the following are communication assets:

- Pitch deck

- One-pager

- Company brochure

- Video pitch

- Website

An asset is more than just a communication vehicle. An asset creates value for your story and amplifies it, often independently of you being there to tell it.

Dedicating time, energy, and money to creating great assets is one of the best investments you can make in the success of your company. There is a lot you can do yourself, but eventually you'll need to hire professionals.

For written material, a copywriter can save you a lot of time by turning your business documents into compelling prose for a website, a script for a video, or a one-pager.

An experienced designer will bring a level of finesse to any PowerPoint presentation. Good design is crucial to convey the value of your idea.

Beauty is truth

People's perception of truth plays a critical role in how seriously they will consider your message, and, ultimately, in their decision about your idea, product, or company. What do we know about truth, and can we anticipate how the audience will perceive our pitch? The answer to that question is linked to the concept of beauty.

Beauty and truth have long been considered two sides of the same coin. The ancient Greeks had a term for that, *kalos kai agathos* – the critical balance of the beautiful (*kalos*) and the good (*agathos*). In medieval art, it was considered inconceivable that something untruthful could be beautiful.

The human propensity for liking and accepting what is perceived as beautiful and elegant is not limited to the arts. On Einstein's theory of relativity, Nobel prize-winning physicist Paul Dirac wrote, "One has great confidence in the theory rising from its great beauty."[31]

An underlying mechanism is at play when people evaluate beauty and truth. Psychologists call it "processing fluency." It describes the subjective ease, or difficulty, of completing a mental task, for example, understanding the strategy on a slide.

Studies have shown that the more fluently or easily we process information, the more positive our aesthetic response. For example, pictures accompanied by matching words (eg, a picture of a dog accompanied by the word "dog") are liked significantly more than pictures accompanied by merely related words (eg, a lock and the word "key"). In turn, these are liked significantly more than pictures accompanied by unrelated words (eg, a desk and the word "snow"). This result is also consistent with people's preference for symmetrical shapes and faces, which are easier to process.[32,33]

dog   key   snow

Processing fluency

Also, information that requires lower processing effort is more likely to be accepted as true, as opposed to information presented in a less accessible form. Thus, a statement clearly printed in dark text against a white background is more likely to be accepted as true than a statement printed in light text against a light background.[34]

Interestingly, the decision to like and trust is almost instantaneous. A study by Google revealed that people consistently rated visually simple websites as more beautiful compared to more visually complex ones and that the decision about whether to stay on a website was taken within one fiftieth to one twentieth of a second.[35]

Ever wondered why Google sticks to such a simple design for its homepage?

Love your slides

We can use this knowledge to our advantage during a presentation. To engage our audience, we can use slides that are simple, clear, and easy to process. We will create a flow and steer away from unnecessary and distracting discussions. Keep this in mind when starting your pitch, where you're introducing a product or launching a new strategy. But you may want to do the opposite, too. If we want to trigger a discussion or questions on specific aspects of our story, we can present those elements in a way that lowers processing fluency, for instance, by making the readability more difficult or increasing information load.

There's a fine balance here. Having only easy-to-process slides might make your audience too passive and lower your perceived value, as the information presented may feel commonplace and self-evident. On the other hand, an overkill of complex information that nobody can even read could lead your audience to doubt your credibility and leave them unconvinced and skeptical.

Start your assets with a slide deck

Whether we like it or not, the PowerPoint presentation has become the expected channel of business communication. Projected, printed, and emailed, millions of slides are created every day to illustrate and discuss all aspects of business, including strategy.

Once your story is ready and it is time for you to create communication assets, a slide deck is the best place to start. Slides are easy to adapt as you improve your presentation based on feedback from your audiences. Other assets are more complex to create and amend, and you often need to hire outside help. Even for slides, you will need to work with a designer to identify the visuals that best reinforce your message and test how to use them most effectively.

Once you have a clear story and a strong pitch deck, it's straightforward to translate that into any other asset, such as content for a website, a company brochure, or a one-pager.

How to present your strategy so your audience remembers it

Study after study has shown that people at all levels of organizations have trouble recalling strategy.[36,37]

Can we improve the impact of our strategy presentations? Researchers studied the effectiveness of different ways of presenting strategy on slides in a realistic and controlled business setting, applying rigorous statistical analysis to interpret the results. You'll love what they found.[38]

The experiment

Three groups of mid-senior managers were given a business strategy presentation, the only variable being how the slides presented the information. The researchers focused on three common approaches to presenting strategy on slides, namely, bullet-point lists, road maps, and visual metaphors.

Bullet points are often the visualization tool of choice in corporate strategy presentations. They are easy to insert and allow for information to be organized in smaller chunks. Probably the most significant limitation of bullet points is that they do not convey connections between pieces of information except for their hierarchy. Additionally, it's tempting to decrease the font size to fit in more text.

Strategy road maps, also called temporal diagrams, are another business presentation favorite. In its simplest form, think of several milestones placed on a timeline. A temporal diagram can simplify the information and deliver it in chronological order. This instantly reveals causal and temporal relationships, which would otherwise require a lengthy – and quickly forgotten – explanation.

Visual metaphors are an even more sophisticated way of conveying complex information. By associating an unfamiliar idea with one that is commonplace, we can spark better understanding of complex ideas. The image of a brick wall can represent a difficult challenge the organization has to overcome. A rowing team on a boat represents the need for internal alignment and cooperation. The most effective metaphors are those that instantly ring true with your audience, without sounding like clichés.

The results

The data analysis revealed that bullet points are by far the worst visualization tool in terms of gaining the audience's attention, their information retention, and their agreement with the strategy. Participants exposed to bullet points reported losing focus during the presentation, failed to recall parts of the strategy and found the strategy less consistent and aligned.

Importantly, the use of different visuals affected how the presenter was perceived by the audience. The presenter armed with bullet points was rated as less prepared, less committed, and less credible than the presenters who used either the road map or a visual metaphor. The audience's perception of visuals is a strong predictor of their perception of the presenter.

These results confirm what we probably all know deep inside, but somehow forget to implement the moment we open PowerPoint: it's time to ditch the bullets for good.

Five easy pitch pieces

There's nothing like a killer presentation to secure fundraising for your startup. But if you're serious about making an impact, you'll need more than one pitch deck.

In fact, there are five fundamental decks that every founder-CEO should have in their arsenal:

1. The teaser deck

2. The three-minute pitch deck

3. The extended pitch deck

4. The master deck

5. The TED deck

Slide types

Three minute pitch deck	Teaser deck	TED deck
Pitch deck	Master deck	

Slide load

Teaser deck   Pitch deck   Master deck

Five decks

The teaser deck

This is your entry-level deck. In most cases, it will be sent by email, and just needs to create enough interest to get a follow-up meeting with investors. Anyone looking at your teaser should be able to grasp what you're trying to say, without you having to say it, and it should only take them a couple of minutes. Think of it like a movie trailer. It needs to generate excitement and interest, without giving away the surprise.

Keep it brief. Explain the problem you're addressing, how your science or technology can help, and add a slide on what's happening in the market. Introduce your stellar team and give a summary of where you are now. No complex science and absolutely no confidential information.

Investors see hundreds of decks like yours every year, so this one needs to stand out from the crowd.

The three-minute pitch deck

This quick-fire pitch deck covers a three- to five-minute presentation. It's the deck you'll use when participating in pitch competitions, or for a brief meeting with investors or prospective partners.

This version should contain all the elements of your main pitch deck (coming up next) but be super lean. You only have a short time, so ensure your key messages jump out on each slide and lose any unnecessary information.

Let your science and technology shine. Pick your best data and make it memorable. But don't give it all away. Think of this as an appetizer. There's plenty more where this came from – leave your audience desperate to hear it.

The extended pitch deck

This is your core deck. It allows you to present your vision, science, technology, team, and business with total clarity. It's what you'll use when you get your first proper presentation with investors and should take fifteen to twenty minutes.

Exactly what to include in the deck is a matter of opinion. Some companies, like Sequoia Capital, have an itemized list of what to include.[39] The basic components however are constant. Investors need to understand your vision, your solution, and your strategy to grow a successful business – including what makes your team ideally placed to make it happen and the challenges that stand in your way.

The sequence really depends on what your strengths are. If you have a truly exceptional team, start by talking about them. If you have a compelling sense of urgency to your story, start there.

You need to help investors understand how great your product is. Share enough scientific data to cover their main concerns. And help them draw conclusions from your data by organizing it around a clear statement. Use the three pillars exercise to help you organize the information.

The master deck

This deck has everything. It's the one you'll use during advanced conversations with investors or prospective partners. These meetings may be with specialists: scientists, product developers, IP lawyers. They'll want to dig deep.

Design is important, but with the master deck, content is king. You will go into great detail about your company, talking about the science, the technology, your patent position, the market, and your competitors. It does not matter how many slides you have, so if you're not sure whether something should be included, add it at the end as a backup slide. You never know if it might be useful.

The TED deck

Your fifth and final deck is the TED deck – as in a TED Talk presentation (which, at eighteen minutes long, is a similar length to your extended pitch deck). But your TED deck will not be the same as your pitch deck, because it will be for a wider audience.

Your story is not always just about the financials and the science. Remember that most successful entrepreneurs are those who excel at creating and sharing inspiring stories about their product, company, and vision. The TED deck allows you to get audiences, especially non-specialist audiences, excited about your big idea and will establish you as a visionary and charismatic leader. Your audience wants to understand where your passion comes from. Why do you care so much? Why should *they* care? Tell them about your vision, how you see the world changing. Share your story. What made you the person you are today? What drove you to start your company?

Your TED deck should be light on content but packed with emotional appeal. It needs to be visually arresting, professional, and carry a clear, simple message. Less is definitely more.

Try using images instead of text to portray your ideas. One strong graphic image or succinct line of text will tell your story much better than a crowded collage or lengthy paragraph. For inspiration for your deck, take a look at the official TEDx guide.[40]

If you have these five decks ready and waiting, you'll be fully prepared whenever opportunity knocks at your door.

INSIDE STORY – WHY YOU NEED NUMBERS IN YOUR PITCH DECK

For a killer fundraising presentation, you need to demonstrate numeracy.

Startups are businesses, and businesses run on numbers. The one thing your presentation should not be is numberless. It's nearly impossible to convey complex numerical arguments with only words. Charts, graphs, and tables are much more efficient ways to do this.

Examples from the movies: Strong openings

Think of your investor pitch like a James Bond movie. Everyone who watches Bond movies loves the opening sequences, before the titles come on. There is suspense, action, amazing stunts. Those first few minutes truly bring home why you love Bond, and that keeps you going through the next two hours of implausible plot twists.

In the same way, you need to convey why an investor should love your business in the first three minutes of your presentation.

Always demo

Seeing is believing. There is a reason why Steve Jobs always demoed his products on stage, sometimes taking risks because the product was still not ready to ship. And indeed, demoing a product requires preparation. Things can go wrong.

Making your product visible is the best way to create credibility. A graph with the activity of your drug is not enough. But what if your product does not exist yet, or it is not visible to the naked eye?

If you are developing drugs, you could use an X-ray photograph of the molecule, an immunofluorescence image, a microscopic photograph of cells or tissue exposed to your product, or even a picture of a tube containing your product, possibly with a clear label identifying the content and your company.

You could even consider creating the ultimate image, a photograph of your product once it is manufactured, labeled, and ready to ship. Of course, you are probably years away from that day, but design can do wonders. Ask your designer to create a mock-up of your product based on what you expect it to look like. The vial, the label, even the box, nicely arranged as if ready to be used. The ultimate FOMO (fear of missing out) weapon.

The most important slide in your deck

Every slide in your pitch deck should feel like an essential component of a perfect recipe for success. Every slide is crucial to support your story, to convince investors that they should put money into your company.

But there is one slide that needs your full attention. This is the first slide, the slide that gets the longest screen time. This is where you need to invest a lot of thinking, time, and design expertise.

Think about it. If you are at a conference and you are the next speaker, the chairperson will announce you like this: "Ladies and gentlemen, the next speaker is the CEO of X and we're going to hear about Y," and there will be your first slide, already on screen. It is still there as you walk to the podium, thank the chairperson, and start introducing yourself. Sometimes that slide is on screen for several minutes.

Or perhaps you're at a board meeting presenting to investors, and you connect your laptop to the projector, and your first slide is there as you're thanking everyone for the invitation. That first slide is your background while you tell them who you are and what you're going to talk about.

Be sure that the first slide makes the most of the opportunity. Give it all the elements your audience needs to understand your message in the most efficient way.

There are several options for an effective first slide. You can use a slide with a plain background, your company name, logo, and value proposition underneath. Clean, clear, and consistent. Another effective option is to add a big image to the first slide that conveys a message about your product, your company, and your vision with your company value proposition and your logo. It should tell your audience what they'll get when they invest in you.

Ideally, you want this first slide to be consistent with your website. Investors might visit your website after the presentation – finding the same messages, visuals, and brand elements there will contribute to their sense of your credibility and professionalism.

Here's what *not* to put on the first slide of your live presentation:

- The date. Who cares?

- "Confidential." If it's a confidential event, that should have been explained beforehand, so the audience will know the content is confidential. If it's an open event, you can't assume anything will be confidential.

- Email addresses, telephone numbers, URLs. They can be provided at the end.

- Legal disclaimers. The only caveat to this comes if you share the slides by email or as a printed document. If that is the case, information about confidentiality is essential.

Make sure your first slide is crisp and clear about who you are, what you do, and how you're going to make the world a better place. Get rid of anything that does not directly support that message.

CASE STUDY – COMMUNICATION ASSETS CONVEY THE VALUE

A young life sciences venture capital firm was preparing to raise a new investment fund. They felt their distinctive approach was not represented in their current fundraising story. They were particularly dissatisfied with their company deck, a clear but otherwise tedious document.

While the management teams of other VC firms in their sector are run by grey-suited bankers or the young-and-fast techies, this team was all about caring for and supporting exceptional scientist founders on their difficult entrepreneurial journey. This was also what they wanted to share with their investors. Their pitch was not about their own results and track record, but a personal story and showcase of each one of their "incredible founders."

They translated the personal character of the narrative to their pitch deck, which contained a personal showcase page for each of the founders and their stories. The newly designed deck looked professional and arresting, significantly contributing to the impact of the story.

The new narrative was embraced by the whole investment team and was incorporated not only in their fundraising story but also in all their other communications material.

Soon after, the firm closed a hugely successful funding round.

EXERCISE – THINK MOVIE POSTER, NOT SLIDE

Movie posters are a great source of inspiration for what a memorable and effective opening slide should look like.

- Choose one movie you have seen recently with a plot that you can remember. Now go online and search for their original movie poster.

- What do you see?
- For example, you could look up the movie poster for *First Man*.[41] You would see:
  - A big, beautiful image: An astronaut, eyes closed, dreaming, the moon.
  - The title, big, across the image: *First Man*.
  - The "presenter": Ryan Gosling.
  - The value proposition: "One giant leap into the unknown."
  - Some other small print and the Universal logo: Small, at the bottom.
- Now think about the value proposition behind your presentation. What would the tagline be if it was a film?
- Come up with a few words (or even one word) that would be your title.
- Find a key image that sums it up.

For an unforgettable opening slide, that should be all you need.

Summary

It's not enough to have a clear story in your head, on a piece of paper, or on a Word document. You need to create communication assets that will help you share the story with investors, and the world. An asset is more than just a communication vehicle. It creates value for your story and amplifies it independently of you being there to tell it. Dedicating time and energy to creating great assets is one of the best investments you can make in the success of your company. And good design is crucial to convey the value of your idea.

The best place to start to create assets is the pitch deck. Slides are easy to change, improve, and adapt, especially if you enlist the help of an expert designer. And once you have a story and a pitch deck, it is straightforward to translate this story into other assets, like a website.

There are five fundamental decks that every founder should have. Besides your extended pitch deck, you need: a shorter version for a teaser presentation, which you'll probably send by email; a three- to five-minute version for a pitching competition or a first meeting; a master deck that contains everything; and a TED deck, for a public presentation along the lines of a TED Talk, which allows you get wider audiences excited about your big idea.

Remember that the first slide is the most important slide in your deck, so focus your efforts there.

EIGHT
Change The World

Having a compelling story is just the beginning of an exciting journey that goes beyond fundraising. Getting the funding you need is only the first step towards growing a successful business and contributing to making the world a healthier place.

Look around you. In today's world, the most successful leaders are not trying to sell a product. They are on a mission to make the world a better place, thanks to their big idea, product, or technology. It's time you let the world know about your mission.

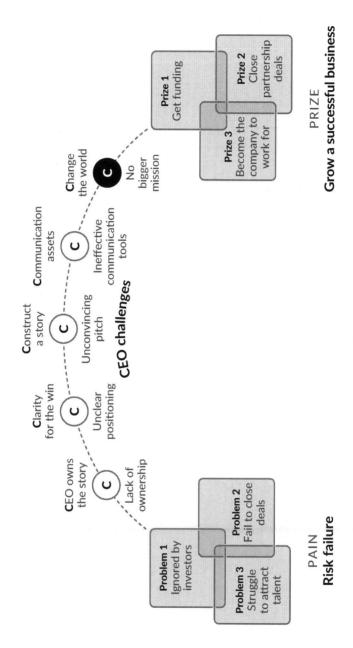

The StoryPitch™ model

The CEO: Chief storyteller

Here we explore the CEO's second responsibility, which arises naturally from the first responsibility of securing funding. That is, the CEO as chief storyteller, the one who is primarily responsible for sharing the company story with the world.

This is particularly important when it comes to the complexity of life sciences. It's one thing to transform science and strategy into a compelling narrative – delivering it with clarity, authority, and passion is another challenge altogether.

As the CEO, you are the person your colleagues, partners, and investors expect to pitch the company's story. This is especially true for investors, who are not only evaluating the narrative, its potential appeal, and its relevance to the current moment. They are also evaluating your ability to share that story in a way that connects with a larger audience.

Seeing a CEO in action during a pitch is an excellent way for investors to assess their leadership and communication skills. As the company's de facto chief spokesperson, the CEO must be enthusiastic, provocative, and comfortable pitching the company's story to prospects and the media while still presenting to investors in future fundraising rounds.

Leverage your story to create value

As CEO, you need to hone your ability to engage with various stakeholders to ensure that your story is heard and embraced. Your communication competency is the focus of attention and is continually being evaluated. Don't fall into the trap of believing the message is more important than the messenger: both must be viewed as appealing, worthwhile, and relevant to create lasting marketplace value.

Every interaction with an investor is an opportunity to support future fundraising. Each meeting with big pharma creates an opening for a partnership. Every executive you connect with outside your company is a potential recruit or an enabler for your company's success. Make the most of these opportunities to develop and expand your story.

The "secret sauce" to any successful enterprise is inspiring the people around you. Storytelling is crucial to this, and there should be ample room on your tool belt for skills that support your ability to inspire others. You might not consider yourself a born storyteller – very few of us are – but you can certainly learn. There's amazing value in the ability of a leader to articulate a compelling story. Don't underinvest time or effort in becoming your company's best presenter, communicator, and chief storyteller.

Learn how to speak with conviction, how to use your body to strengthen your message, and how to use your voice to connect emotionally with your audience. And learn to be authentic. Embrace failure. Nobody believes in heroes who always win. We love heroes who try, sometimes fail, and often lose hope, but always try again. Search out the wisdom of entrepreneurial storytellers like Elon Musk, Steve Jobs, and Richard Branson. Get a coach if you think it will help you. Being a "good speaker" is not the goal – being a good *person* who can speak convincingly is what it's really about.

Delivery is key

Working on your delivery goes alongside crafting the content of your story. No matter how good your story is, how you present it will make all the difference between a good pitch and an unforgettable experience that drives your audience to action.

There are endless sources of information on presentation skills. Although it's beyond the purpose of this book, it's essential to be aware of the five key aspects to consider:

1. The expression on your **face** is the first thing your audience will notice. There is a reason why we put so much value on face-to-face meetings. Use different expressions to support the various

emotions of the presentation. Smile, open your eyes wider, raise your eyebrows a little. As in a conversation with a friend, you want your facial expressions to align with the tone of your words and the information you are presenting. The size of the space and your distance to the audience also matters. A bigger crowd requires more prominent facial expressions.

2. Making **eye** contact is essential to grab the attention of your audience. Ensure you look at everyone – that might mean every individual if you have a small audience, or every section of a crowd. Make it a brief glance, not prolonged eye contact that might be intimidating. Let them know that you pay attention and care about how your message is being received. Keep your gaze moving and engage as many people as possible.

3. Your **voice** is a powerful tool to drive the message home. Your voice contributes to the overall impact of your presentation. By making it easier for your listeners to receive your message, you strengthen its significance. Speak in a firm voice, without wavering or trailing off at the ends of sentences. If you are not sure that a word or phrase is worth saying, don't say it. If it is worth saying, say it with enthusiasm and conviction.

4. Your **body** posture, gestures, and movement – that is, the way you stand, move around, and use your hands – set the tone for the whole presentation.

Each situation is different. The key is to set the right tone for the given situation. A formal pitch in a boardroom is different from a keynote presentation at a conference. But remember, exaggerated hand gestures and over-rehearsed movements on stage are off-putting to most audiences.

5. Finally, your **clothes** are an essential component of how you come across. Because the first impression is so important, it is best to dress professionally and in a manner that complements both your personal brand and the character of the event you are speaking at.

Depending on the context of your presentation, you'll need to rely more on some of these five elements. The impact of movement and posture is limited in a Zoom presentation, when eye contact, voice, and facial expression are your best tools. On the contrary, facial expressions and eye contact are less effective with a large audience of hundreds of people, who will be more attentive to your tone of voice and movement on stage.

Although hiring a professional coach to help you master presentation skills is the most effective method, you can do plenty of other things yourself to take your presentation skills to the next level. In the Resources section of this book, you will find a selection of helpful information.

Origin stories

An origin story is a narrative about the establishment of your organization. It sets out your character and ambition, be it the story of an empire, a company, or an individual. It helps you to be remembered – just like the stories we've passed down through the centuries. A great origin story makes it much easier for people to engage with your company.

A story of twin brothers

A long time ago, twin baby boys were born to a princess. The king – her uncle – had stolen the throne from her father. He was afraid that one day, the twins would overthrow him and take the throne back. So he had the boys put into the river in a basket, expecting them to drown. However, the boys were saved thanks to a she-wolf, who fed them until they were found by a herdsman who took them in. They grew up, killed the usurper king, and later founded the city of Rome.

Of course, this is the well-known story of Romulus and Remus. It's also the origin story of the Roman Empire. An image of the brothers being suckled by the she-wolf has been its symbol since ancient times. It tells a narrative of divine origin, strength, courage, leadership, and justice in a story that has endured for centuries.

Per aspera ad astra

"Through adversity to the stars." Most of us come from humble beginnings or have had to overcome obstacles early in our lives, and we love it when successful people reveal they have too. It makes us feel hopeful to know that Richard Branson was a high school dropout before starting Virgin Records as a mail-order record company.[42]

Origin stories reflect, embody, or project the social values and structures of the people who remember and retell them. Not surprisingly, the most successful companies out there have origin stories that are powerful and inspiring to their clients, partners, and employees.

A couple of millennia after Romulus and Remus, a twenty-one-year-old college dropout in Los Altos, California, was hanging out with two friends in his family's garage. It sounds like the beginning of a rock band, but these guys had other things on their mind. Steve Jobs and Ronald Wayne had worked together at video game company Atari, while Steve Wozniak had worked for Hewlett-Packard. The three went on to incorporate Apple Computer on 1 April 1976.[43]

Around the same time, another great company was being founded. In the early 1970s, two scientists pioneered a new scientific field called recombinant DNA technology. When he heard about this development, young venture capitalist Robert Swanson called one of the scientists behind the study. He invited Herbert

Boyer to meet with him, and though it was only meant to be a ten-minute meeting, it lasted over three hours. By its conclusion, legendary innovator Genentech was born, and became the first health and life sciences company to go public.[44]

One of the best documented origin stories is that of healthcare giant Johnson & Johnson. In the early 1860s, the casualties of the American Civil War led Robert Wood Johnson to develop an interest in healthcare. Aged only sixteen when the war began, he was too young to serve with his two older brothers, so he worked in the family pharmacy and developed medicated plasters. Johnson & Johnson has created a beautiful and truly immersive online portal that tells this story about how they became one of today's leading healthcare companies over the last one and a half centuries.[45]

Let them know you: The social media story

Would you buy a Rolex watch from a street vendor in the park? Probably not. It's perfectly fine to buy a sandwich or an ice cream, maybe even a T-shirt or scarf, from a street vendor, but for a more serious investment, we need evidence that the vendor won't rip us off.

Having a product is not enough. People don't do business with just anyone. They do business with people they know, like, and trust. This principle is a natural law of business in all its aspects. Consumers only buy products from brands they know, like, and trust. Talented people want to work for companies they know, like, and trust.

The same is true in fundraising. You can't expect to walk into the boardroom with your flashy pitch deck and have investors deposit a few million into your company's bank account just like that. Doing business together is a matter of trust. Building trust takes time, and it always starts with knowing and liking someone.

There's a big difference between knowing about someone and really knowing them. For example, I can say I know a lot about a famous person. I am a big fan of the actress Uma Thurman. I've seen a lot of her movies and I've read interviews with her. I have read up on not only her career, but her personal life, her relationships, her family, and even her political views. And yet, that's not enough for me to say I know her. What would it take to know the real Uma Thurman, rather than just knowing about her?

The difference between knowing about someone and knowing someone is direct personal communication. You only know someone when he or she actively shares information with you, especially intimate, private information. This is why it feels special to know someone instead of just knowing about them. They have opened up to you personally.

If Uma Thurman tells only me about her favorite movie instead of mentioning it in a magazine interview read by millions, that means she's deemed me worthy of sharing that information, which means I appreciate it. And when it comes to more sensitive information, personal communication comes with a lot of trust and vulnerability. Just think about how much it means when someone tells you, "You're the only person I've ever told this to."

The different ways in which we can "know" someone were originally described by the philosopher David Matheson of Carleton University.[46] Matheson calls the knowledge we might have about a celebrity impersonal knowledge, while the kind that would lead to you saying you know someone he calls personal knowledge.

At the time he wrote the essay, personal knowledge was only limited to people you knew directly. But in the past decade, social media has exploded, so that you can now access the kind of personal information about famous people that you never would have had access to in the past. I can go to Uma Thurman's Instagram profile and follow her to get a personal and detailed account of her life. Of course, she has over a million followers, but the magic of social media is that it still feels personal. The twentieth century was about impersonal mass communication, mass advertising, and mass selling. Now the business pendulum has swung towards up-close and personal.

If you are serious about your story, it should be reflected in your social media presence. Social media is a convenient and effective way to share your story. Let investors get to *know* you, not just about you. The information in your pitch, a press release, a company website, even an interview in a high-profile magazine is not enough. You need to offer your audience a consistent flow of insights into your entrepreneurial journey.

How to write your origin story

When you write your origin story, there are three things you need to do:

1. Choose what's relevant. Make sure you only focus on what's most important in your narrative. Even if it's true, it might not be necessary for the story. It does not matter whether Steve Jobs liked cycling or eating cornflakes. It matters that he dropped out of college.[47]

2. Keep it real. Never make up an origin story. When Richard Branson dropped out of school, his plan wasn't to create the mammoth Virgin empire. But it's fascinating to know that he had started a youth culture magazine aged fifteen, as it aligns to Branson's passion to drive positive change in the world.[48]

3. Be personal. Origin stories are compelling because they speak to us about struggle, pain, and hard times. Don't skip the sections about your tough early years because you are the CEO now. People are interested in the things that affect them too. So, tell them how you struggled, what you were willing to fight for, and why your business is all so personal to you.

My origin story

Or, how I learned to stop worrying and love the story.

As far back as I can remember, I always wanted to be a movie director. Even as a child, I was drawn by the allure of captivating the audience, the chance to make an impact, or maybe just the thrill of creating an inspiring story.

I grew up in Italy and my family lived near a park, which was home to an open-air cinema every summer. In June, workers would spend a week installing rows of metal stools in the main square, a wooden ticket office near the entrance, and a magnificent big screen. And then, on the Saturday of the big opening, a film would show. And every evening for the rest of the summer, a new one would follow. It was glorious. Or, it would have been, if any of us kids could afford it.

We couldn't let the opportunity to see those films slip by – so we hatched a plan. At dusk, we'd hide in the bushes surrounding the cinema. Then, once the lights were off, we'd sneak inside.

It felt like an operation by the Marines. We would spread out, hiding in different areas, to mitigate risk. We wore dark clothes for camouflage. We calculated our steps so just one group, in one area, would move in at a time. We kept our heads low, voices hushed, and fingers crossed – all hoping that we wouldn't get caught. Hoping that we'd get to catch the movie of the day.

And somehow, incredibly, we did. Frequently. We'd hold our breath as soon as we got inside, waiting for the flash of a torch in our direction, but it rarely came. Instead, we'd be left with our fast-beating hearts, our smug smiles at having outsmarted the grown-ups, and the glory of the films.

Of course, later in life, I learned that the cinema owner had known about our operations the whole time. He had let us watch the movies anyway: *Jaws*, *Alien*, *ET*, *Star Wars*, *Rocky*, *The Godfather*, *Mad Max* – it was bliss.

Until my own story took a turn.

After one particularly exciting summer of films, my parents got divorced. We moved to a new home, far away from my neighborhood friends and the park, and the open-air cinema faded into a distant memory. Life entered the fast lane. I got a PhD, had a family and a mortgage, and was working for a big corporation in a serious role. I'd become a grown-up.

But even though I was older, and that I was now living even further away from that neighborhood park (all the way over in Amsterdam, to be precise), I still felt my heart speed up when I watched a good movie. And I still felt the desire to create stories of my own.

It seemed like the more adult I became, and the more responsibilities I accrued, the louder that dream got in my mind. But it was a crazy dream. Right?

I couldn't throw away a gratifying job, the years I'd spent working towards my PhD, or my family's stability. I couldn't put everything on the line – everything I'd spent my life working for – to chase a childhood aspiration. That would be reckless. That would be wild. That would be a risk that no one in their right mind could take. Wouldn't it? It all came down to one day in New York City. I was there for business and had planned to attend a workshop by Robert McKee, one of the most sought-after screenwriting lecturers in the world. I knew his lecture would give me information about the craft. But what it ended up giving me was so much more.

Because, while McKee spoke about screenwriting, he also talked about the power of storytelling. How the art and science of great stories – the principles, methods, and insights from the most successful movies – can be applied to bring value to anything. Even, and especially, business.

I was energized. Ecstatic. Bewildered . . . and ready for action!

On that day, in that workshop, I decided to put my childhood dream to work. I decided to dedicate my career to storytelling for businesses, transforming great ideas and products into unforgettable narratives. First, I practiced in the company where I was already working. Then, a couple of years later, I founded my own company.

Today, I use classic storytelling techniques from the movies to create powerful business narratives that excite audiences in the same way that they excited me as a child. (Ask any of my clients, and they'll tell you how often I use classic film examples in my workshops. Hint: it's often.)

I discovered as a child that the power of a great story is limitless, and I still experience that today. OK, I didn't get to become a Hollywood director. But I still get to wake up every day and create stories about amazing ideas, technologies, and companies that will make the world a better place. And I get to experience the thrill of helping my clients inspire audiences and create a lasting impact on them.

And to me, that's what my childhood dream was all about.

CASE STUDY - CHANGE THE WORLD

Fundraising pitches often use a patient's story but fail to get the attention of the audience. The tale sounds impersonal, artificial, not credible, and forced. Unless it's a real personal story close to the heart of the presenter, that is.

The CEO of a biotech startup operating in the healthy aging field was preparing to raise their first seed round. The drugs they were developing were not particularly novel, but their approach was. Instead of creating new medicines from scratch, they wanted to find existing and already approved drugs that could be used to treat age-related diseases, to get the drugs to the patients as quickly as possible.

This sense of urgency was reinforced by the personal mission of the founder and CEO, who had experienced first-hand the pain and consequences of age-related disease when a family member's health started to deteriorate.

The solutions the company wanted to develop were too late for the CEO's father but not for the current aging generation. The combination of the personal story with a clear strategy aiming at an accelerated approval convinced the investors, who granted first Series A funding followed a by a successful double-digit million-dollar Series B round.

Summary

You've worked hard with your team and now you have a compelling company story, ready to be shared with the world. The most important part of your job as CEO starts now.

You are the person your colleagues, partners, and investors expect to share the company's story – especially investors. They want to see you in action, because this is an excellent way for them to assess your leadership and communication skills. You are the de facto chief spokesperson of the company. Your efforts and communication competency are continually being evaluated.

Few of us are born storytellers or presenters. But there's always time to learn. Don't underestimate the value you will get from being a storyteller. Invest time and effort in becoming your company's best communicator. It will pay dividends.

And don't forget to share your story on social media, which is such an important tool to get your voice heard. Remember, investors don't just buy good products. They buy them from people they know, like, and trust. Building trust starts well before you enter the boardroom or the meeting room. Social media is a very convenient place to start.

An effective way to build trust is by having an origin story that establishes your organization, its character, and its ambition. Keep it personal and be honest about the times when you have had to overcome failures. Nobody wants to hear about a company that is always winning. Don't leave out the struggle. That is what audiences find compelling.

NINE
Storytelling Like A Pro

Reading the theory behind great pitches is fine, but nothing teaches you better than seeing the real thing. For me, Elon Musk's 2015 presentation for the Tesla Powerwall launch did everything a good story should do. Musk did a fantastic job by sharing a compelling and convincing story for his product, a new type of rechargeable battery. Many seasoned observers of tech pitches called it "the best tech keynote" they had ever seen.[49,50]

It is worth analyzing the pitch in depth. Let's use what we've learned in this book to understand how he did it.

Elon Musk's Tesla Powerwall pitch

Opening

As Musk walks on stage, there is one slide with Tesla's logo. Musk introduces himself with the key message of his presentation: "Tonight is about a fundamental transformation of how the world works, how energy is delivered across the Earth." This is also the mission of Tesla, "to accelerate the world's transition to sustainable energy."

The three-act structure

He clearly uses the classical three-act structure and breaks it down for his audience.

Act 1: Set-up

Musk shows a set of images of the impact of using fossil fuels for energy accompanied by the phrase "This is real." He replies to someone in the audience with, "This is how it is today. It's pretty bad. It sucks."

These statements are simple, uncomplicated. We cannot deny this. We are familiar with this situation and it is urgent.

Act 2: Surprise, shift, struggle

Musk uses a graph to show the growth of carbon dioxide concentration in the atmosphere. He explains the curve and how every year the concentration is increasing. He forecasts how bad it will get if this continues unabated.

The message is clear – the world is heading towards a very bad place. What's more, in 2015, public awareness of the evidence of global warming was lower, so this would have been all the more shocking.

Act 3: Solution, climax

Musk presents the solution, which happens to be there in the sky above us. It's the sun, nature's fusion reactor. The answer is solar energy, not batteries. And it can be done! Musk explains how all fossil fuel can be replaced by using relatively small land mass and rooftops.

At this climax, Musk finally introduces "the missing piece" – the Tesla Powerwall.

The three dimensions of the problem

Musk goes on to address all three dimensions of the problem, ie, the Earth's dependence on fossil fuels, to increase the audience's engagement.

The philosophical problem

Note that Musk starts with the big problem, the reason for Tesla to exist, the "why." He describes how we

WINNERS HAVE A STORY

are destroying the world, how our use of fossil fuel is making our planet a very bad place to be for us and for all living things.

The practical problem

In our own everyday life, current batteries suck, and Musk gives multiple reasons why. This describes to the audience a real, concrete, relatable problem.

The personal problem

Here Musk implicates us all in the problem. We are all using up fossil fuels and contributing to catastrophic climate change, and this is not just a problem for us. We are destroying the planet for the rest of the creatures that inhabit it.

He appeals to us on an emotional level, underlining that Tesla and the audience share the same values and concerns.

The audience as the hero

Musk knows he cannot save the planet personally, nor can his product, nor Tesla. But the audience can, by buying his products. Investors can, by supporting his company and mission. Governments can, by embracing this approach, encouraging the setting-up of Gigafactories. He makes the audience the hero of the story. And who would not like to be at the center of such a great story, with a mission to save the planet?

Musk's tenor is humble. He speaks to the audience with a frank tone that doesn't feel manipulative or canned. He's having an honest conversation about how a new product might solve a major problem. And he is serious about this. Tesla has already opened some of its patents to competitors, and he announces that it will even open its Gigafactory plans to others.

The power of three

Musk does not go deeply into the technology, but he does make sure the key aspects of his product are clear. And there are three advantages in particular that he wants us to remember:

1. Convenience: The product is wall mounted. It does not require a special facility or its own room.

2. Peace of mind: Even if other power sources fail, you'll have this one.

3. Affordability: It's €3500.

Show it

We don't want only graphs and calculations. We want to see the real thing. Musk provides this at several points during his presentation. First, he uses an image of the Powerwall and a video illustrating how it will work. Second, he physically displays the products. They come in a range of colors, and are visually appealing. Their design gives them the look of an artistic sculpture. Remember how beauty reinforces credibility?

Finally, Musk reveals that the entire presentation and the venue has been powered by his product, completely off the grid. How cool is that?

All this in under twenty minutes

Musk closes his eighteen-minute presentation with a strong call to action: To end dependence on fossil fuels.

Summary

The application of the storytelling principles described in this book can turn a complicated technology pitch into an inspiring story that gets your audience excited and ready to commit to your mission.

This is clearly demonstrated in Elon Musk's Tesla Powerwall presentation, considered by many as the start of Musk's stratospheric success and one of the best technology pitches ever delivered.

And the beauty of it? You can do it, too.

Conclusion

Congratulations on reading *Winners Have a Story* and taking the first and most important steps towards turning your science and technology into a compelling story. You're on your way to getting funded, growing a successful business, and making the world a healthier place.

Success often starts with a great story, in business and in life. We have discussed the importance of a story and why every fundraising CEO needs one, because crafting and sharing your story is one of the essential steps to grow a successful company.

Your story doesn't need to be entertaining, because "story" is not synonymous with "entertainment." Your story is a tool to structure your company narrative in a way that clarifies the strategy and conveys the value of your big idea, your product, and your company.

And your company story today is based on the same elements that have been used for millennia and still form the basis for every successful novel, book, and film. Stories are compelling because they connect the logical and emotional brains of your audience – including investors.

Stories are not pitches. When you pitch, it's because you want something from your audience: their attention, their time, their money. When you tell a story, you give them something. You share a gift with the audience, something extraordinary – an idea, a new insight, a new vision for the world that they didn't have before.

Clarity in your narrative is the driving force of success. Why is the world better off with the existence of your company? What is the significant change in the world that makes your company so relevant today? What is the problem your company is solving? Not just the practical problem, not just the biological pathway your drug is inhibiting or the receptor your antibodies are activating. What is the bigger problem, the philosophical problem? And be aware of the personal, emotional problem of your audience. Only by addressing the three problems together will you make your story compelling.

Don't be afraid of mentioning your challenges. We don't want to hear only about the heroes who always win. The heroes we love are those who try, fail, and stand up again.

The best stories are based on a well-honed and proven structure, the three-act structure. You want to construct something that the audience can grasp and get excited about. This will make your work immensely easier.

Remember that you are not the hero of the story. *You* are not going to solve cancer. *You* are not going to eliminate diseases. Not unless investors put money in your company. Not unless pharma companies partner with your startup to help you develop your product and bring it to the market. Not unless doctors and nurses use your products. *They* are the heroes of your story.

Finally, make sure that your story has the means to spread around the world. Your first communication asset should be a kick-ass pitch deck in various forms. The pitch deck is your most valuable tool on the journey to getting funded. It should combine logic and emotion, design and structure, content and form.

Once you have created your story and the assets that will make your story spread in the world, it's time to take on your ultimate responsibility as CEO. It's time to become your company's chief storyteller.

Don't expect it to be a smooth road. You will find many obstacles on the way to the creation and implementation of your story. Your most trusted advisers might tell you to stick to the science. If you are a scientist yourself, you might feel that data and not a story should drive your pitch, especially if you don't have the time and the support to create a compelling story, or if you're developing a problem that is years away from the market.

If you can address all these doubts and cope with this struggle, you are well poised to make a dent in the universe. Your story will start circulating. First, internally. Then with investors. Later, in your sector and perhaps the press. Because this is the magic of the story. It spreads exponentially, like the ripples of a stone thrown in the lake.

Next steps

If you follow the principles and the StoryPitch™ method described in this book, you will be able to create a compelling story for your science, product, and company. This story will serve you as your most valuable fundraising tool without wasting your precious time and energy in the process. I have given you all you need, but if the thought of going it alone scares you, consider enlisting professional support. People like me are here to help you tell your story.

And now, time for action.

Winners have a story. What's yours?

References

1 P Meath, "Life Sciences Outlook 2021: The evolution continues for startup funding," J.P.Morgan (2021), www.jpmorgan.com/commercial-banking/insights/life-sciences-startup-outlook, data used with permission

2 Used with permission from Google Books Ngram Viewer, https://books.google.com/ngrams

3 R Branson, "Why entrepreneurs are storytellers," Virgin (9 February 2016), www.virgin.com/branson-family/richard-branson-blog/why-entrepreneurs-are-storytellers, accessed 5 March 2022

4 C Jung, J Campbell (ed.), *The Portable Jung* (Penguin Books, 1976), p178

5   AR Damasio, *Descartes' Error: Emotion, reason, and the human brain* (Penguin Books, 2005)

6   D Ariely, *Predictably Irrational: The hidden forces that shape our decisions* (HarperCollins Canada, 2008)

7   E Musk, "Making humans a multiplanetary species" (2016), www.youtube.com/ watch?v=H7Uyfqi_TE8, accessed 5 March 2022

8   E Musk, "Making life multiplanetary" (2017), www.youtube.com/watch?v=tdUX3ypDVwI, accessed 5 March 2022

9   JF Kennedy, "Address at Rice University on the nation's space effort, 12 September 1962," John F Kennedy Presidential Library and Museum, www.jfklibrary.org/learn/about-jfk/historic-speeches/address-at-rice-university-on-the-nations-space-effort, accessed 5 March 2022

10 B Horowitz, "How Andreessen Horowitz evaluates CEOs," a16z (31 May 2010), https:// a16z.com/2010/05/31/how-andreessen-horowitz-evaluates-ceos, accessed 5 March 2022

11 Aristotle, W Rhys Roberts (trans.), *Rhetoric, vol. 1, The Internet Classics Archive*, http://classics. mit.edu/Aristotle/rhetoric.1.i.html, accessed 5 March 2022

12 D Daily, *The Classic Treasury of Aesop's Fables* (Running Press Kids, 2007)

13 K Robinson, "Do schools kill creativity?" February 2006, TED, www.ted.com/talks/ sir_ken_robinson_do_schools_kill_creativity, accessed 5 March 2022

14 S Jobs, "Keynote address" (Macworld Conference and Expo, 2007), https://podcasts.apple.com/us/podcast/macworld-san-francisco-2007-keynote-address/id275834665?i=1000026524322, accessed 5 March 2022

15 E Musk, "Tesla introduces Tesla Energy" (2015), www.youtube.com/watch?v=NvCIhn7_FXI, accessed 5 March 2022

16 B Horowitz, *The Hard Thing About Hard Things: Building a business when there are no easy answers* (Harper Business, 2014)

17 J Jordan, "Investing in Neighbor," a16z (30 January 2020), https://a16z.com/2020/01/30/neighbor, accessed 5 March 2022

18 A Hilaly, "How to present to investors," Sequoia Capital (no date), https://articles.sequoiacap.com/how-to-present-to-investors, accessed 5 March 2022

19 J Birkinshaw, "Telling a good innovation story," McKinsey Quarterly (19 July 2018), www.mckinsey.com/featured-insights/innovation-and-growth/telling-a-good-innovation-story, accessed 5 March 2022

20 A Raskin, "Great pitches start with change," Medium (5 December 2017), https://medium.com/the-mission/great-pitches-start-with-change-2c7e696b86ea, accessed 5 March 2022

21 E Greenberg, M Hirt, and S Smit, "The global forces inspiring a new narrative of progress," McKinsey Quarterly (6 April 2017), www.

mckinsey.com / business-functions / strategy-
and-corporate-finance / our-insights / the-global-
forces-inspiring-a-new-narrative-of-progress,
accessed 5 March 2022

22 R McKee, *Story: Substance, structure, style and the
principles of screenwriting* (HarperCollins, 2010)

23 R Pausch, "The Last Lecture: Really achieving
your childhood dreams," Carnegie Mellon
University (18 September 2007), www.youtube.
com / watch?v=ji5_MqicxSo, accessed 5 March
2022

24 R Pausch and J Zaslow, *The Last Lecture: Lessons
in living* (Two Roads, 2008)

25 S Spielberg, *Jaws* (Universal Pictures, 1975)

26 Q Tarantino, *Kill Bill: Volume 1* (A Band Apart,
2003)

27 K Johnson, *The Incredible Hulk* (Universal
Television, 1977)

28 D Barrymore, *Whip It* (Mandate Pictures and
Flower Films, 2009)

29 Homer, E Rieu (trans.), *The Odyssey* (Penguin
Books, 2003)

30 KA Carlson and SB Shu, "When three charms
but four alarms: Identifying the optimal number
of claims in persuasion settings," SSRN, (2013),
https: / / ssrn.com / abstract=2277117, accessed 5
March 2022

31 P Dirac, Quoted in J McAllister, *Beauty and
Revolution in Science* (Cornell University Press,
1999)

32 N Schwarz, H Song, and J Xu, "When thinking is difficult: Metacognitive experiences as information," in M Wänke, *The Social Psychology of Consumer Behavior* (Psychology Press, 2009), pp201–223

33 R Reber, N Schwarz, and P Winkielman, "Processing fluency and aesthetic pleasure: Is beauty in the perceiver's processing experience?" *Personality and Social Psychology Review*, 8/4 (2004), 364–382, https://doi.org/10.1207/s15327957pspr0804_3

34 R Reber and N Schwarz, "Effects of perceptual fluency on judgments of truth," *Consciousness and Cognition*, 8/3 (1999), 338–342, https://doi.org/10.1006/ccog.1999.0386

35 AN Tuch, "The role of visual complexity and prototypicality regarding first impression of websites: Working towards understanding aesthetic judgments," *International Journal of Human-Computer Studies*, 70/11 (2012), 794–811, https://doi.org/10.1016/j.ijhcs.2012.06.003

36 RS Kaplan and DP Norton, "The office of strategy management," *Harvard Business Review* (October 2005), https://hbr.org/2005/10/the-office-of-strategy-management, accessed 5 March 2022

37 DJ Collis and MG Rukstad, "Can you say what your strategy is?" *Harvard Business Review* (April 2008), https://hbr.org/2008/04/can-you-say-what-your-strategy-is, accessed 5 March 2022

38 S Kernbach, M Eppler, and S Bresciani, "The use of visualization in the communication of business strategies: An experimental evaluation," *International Journal of Business Communication*, 52/2 (2015), 164–187, https://doi.org/10.1177/2329488414525444

39 Team Sequoia Capital, "Writing a business plan," Sequoia Capital (no date), https://articles.sequoiacap.com/writing-a-business-plan, accessed 5 March 2022

40 TED, "Create + prepare slides," TED (no date), www.ted.com/participate/organize-a-local-tedx-event/tedx-organizer-guide/speakers-program/prepare-your-speaker/create-prepare-slides, accessed 5 March 2022

41 D Chazelle, *First Man* (Universal Pictures, 2018)

42 R Branson, *Losing My Virginity: How I've survived, had fun, and made a fortune doing business my way* (Times Books, 1998)

43 W Isaacson, *Steve Jobs: The exclusive biography* (Little, Brown, 2011)

44 Genentech, "Our founders," Genentech (no date), www.gene.com/about-us/leadership/our-founders, accessed 5 March 2022

45 Johnson & Johnson, "Our story," Johnson & Johnson (no date), https://ourstory.jnj.com, accessed 5 March 2022

46 D Matheson, "Knowing persons," *Dialogue*, 49/3 (2010), 435–453, https://doi.org/10.1017/S0012217310000466

47 W Isaacson, *Steve Jobs: The exclusive biography* (Little, Brown, 2011)

48 R Branson, *Losing My Virginity: How I've survived, had fun, and made a fortune doing business my way* (Times Books, 1998)

49 TC Sottek, "Watch Elon Musk announce Tesla Energy in the best tech keynote I've ever seen," The Verge (1 May 2015), www.theverge.com/2015/5/1/8527543/elon-musk-tesla-battery-feels, accessed 5 March 2022

50 C Gallo, "Tesla's Elon Musk lights up social media with a TED style keynote," *Forbes* (4 May 2015), www.forbes.com/sites/carminegallo/2015/05/04/teslas-elon-musk-lights-up-social-media-with-a-ted-style-keynote/?sh=69864d577ad2, accessed 5 March 2022

Resources

The following sources are recommended as general supplementary reading:

- C Gallo, "'Your Story Is Your Strategy' says VC who backed Facebook and Twitter," *Forbes* (29 April 2014), www.forbes.com/sites/carminegallo/2014/04/29/your-story-is-you r-strategy-says-vc-who-backed-facebook-and-twitter/?sh=4f1347b11dd8, accessed 5 March 2022

- G Kittel, et al, *Theological Dictionary of the New Testament* (Wm B Eerdmans Publishing, 1985)

Andy Raskin is an undisputed world-class leader of strategic storytelling. His articles are an endless source of inspiration and insights for anybody willing to learn about creating a strategic narrative and aligning a company behind it.

Some of my favorites are:

- A Raskin, "To create a new category, name the new game," Medium (17 October 2019), https://medium.com/firm-narrative/to-create-a-new-category-name-the-new-game-70c2e55edc2e, accessed 5 March 2022

- A Raskin, "The greatest sales deck I've ever seen," Medium (15 September 2016), https://medium.com/the-mission/the-greatest-sales-deck-ive-ever-seen-4f4ef3391ba0, accessed 5 March 2022

- A Raskin, "Great pitches start with change," Medium (5 December 2017), https://medium.com/the-mission/great-pitches-start-with-change-2c7e696b86ea, accessed 5 March 2022

Nancy Duarte has written some of the most influential and yet practical books on how to craft, design, and deliver presentations that change the world.

These two books are a great source of inspiration to learn how to leverage techniques normally reserved for cinema and literature to transform any presentation into an engaging journey:

- N Duarte and P Sanchez, *Illuminate: Ignite change through speeches, stories, ceremonies, and symbols*

(Portfolio, 2016) – for leaders who want to inspire people to go after their vision.

- N Duarte, *Resonate: Present visual stories that transform audiences* (John Wiley and Sons, 2010)

Her TEDx presentation on The Secret Structure of Great Talks has been watched almost 3 million times:

- N Duarte, "The secret structure of great talks," November 2011, TED, www.ted.com/talks/ nancy_duarte_the_secret_structure_of_great_ talks?language=en, accessed 5 March 2022

On TED presentations, Chris Anderson's book uses examples from some of the best TED Talks and is a great resource for anyone interested in improving their presentation literacy.

- C Anderson, *TED Talks: The official TED guide to public speaking* (HMH Books, 2017)

More TED Talks on delivering a powerful presentation:

- J Treasure, "How to speak so that people want to listen," June 2013, TED, www.ted.com/talks/ julian_treasure_how_to_speak_so_that_people_ want_to_listen, accessed 5 March 2022
- A Cuddy, "Your body language may shape who you are," June 2012, TED, www.ted.com/talks/

amy_cuddy_your_body_language_may_shape_
who_you_are, accessed 5 March 2022

Carmine Gallo's book *Talk Like TED* is a brilliant guide to public speaking, based on scientific analysis of hundreds of TED presentations and interviews with TED speakers.

- C Gallo, *Talk Like TED: The 9 public speaking secrets of the world's top minds* (St Martin's Press, 2014)

For the Dutch-speaking among us, Theo Hendriks is simply the best corporate storyteller of the Netherlands. All of his books are inspiring and packed with great insights on storytelling in business. *The Wow Starts Now* and *Change the Script* are two of my favorites:

- T Hendriks, *The Wow Starts Now* (Lev., 2018)

- T Hendriks, *Change the Script* (Lev., 2014)

On our website chiaro.nl you will find a collection of free resources including blog posts, articles, and tools to inspire you and make your storytelling journey easy and effective.

Acknowledgments

I am indebted to all the exceptional life sciences entrepreneurs, company founders, and CEOs I have had the pleasure of working with over the years. Thank you for making me part of your journey, your vision, your story. Your passion for turning science into innovative treatments for patients has been a constant source of inspiration for my work.

I wish to thank Florence Allouche, Ann Beliën, Theo Hendriks, Remberto Martis, Christina Takke, Dinko Valerio, and Felice Verduyn-van Weegen for critically reviewing my manuscript. Your candid feedback and your insights have been invaluable in turning my draft manuscript into a book.

And a final thank you to my supportive wife and family. *Grazie* for encouraging me in my own entrepreneurial journey to build a business born of love for great movies. That's a wrap!

The Author

Giuseppe grew up in Italy, where his childhood dream was to be a film director, or something else that involved seeing films, lots of them. Instead, he became a scientist, obtaining a PhD in molecular genetics and working in academic research and biotech.

His lifelong fascination with how successful stories work led him into strategic communications, first at Dutch biotech company Crucell and then at Johnson & Johnson. In his role, he created presentations about science, strategy, and vision for the leaders of one of the world's largest healthcare companies.

More recently, he founded Chiaro, a communications agency specializing in strategic storytelling for the health and life sciences industry. Its clients include some of the most admired organizations of the sector, from biotech to VCs to big pharma.

Giuseppe's mission is to ensure exceptional entrepreneurs get the funding and resources they need to bring their big ideas successfully into the world.

And in case you were wondering, *chiaro* is Italian for "clear and understandable," and "bright and brilliant."

Giuseppe currently lives in the Netherlands.

🌐 www.chiaro.nl

in www.linkedin.com/in/strategic-storytelling-for-healthcare